The Dilemma
of Narcissus

Other titles in the CLASSIC REPRINT series:

Song and Its Fountains   AE

Nature, Contemplation, and the One   John N. Deck

Plotinus: The Enneads   translated by Stephen MacKenna

The Dilemma of Narcissus

Louis Lavelle

Translated from the French
with Introduction and Notes by

W. T. Gairdner
M.A. (Oxon.)
Docteur de l'Université de Paris

CLASSIC
REPRINT
SERIES

PUBLISHED FOR THE PAUL BRUNTON
PHILOSOPHIC FOUNDATION BY

Larson Publications

Originally published in French as *L'Erreur de Narcisse*,
by Editions Bernard Grasset, Paris © 1939

First published in English
by George Allen and Unwin Ltd 1973
This translation © 1973 George Allen and Unwin Ltd
Used by permission of HarperCollins Publishers Limited

This edition © 1993 by Larson Publications/
Paul Brunton Philosophic Foundation

International Standard Book Number (cloth) 0-943914-61-2
International Standard Book Number (paper) 0-943914-62-0
Library of Congress Catalog Card Number: 93-77049

Published for the Paul Brunton Philosophic Foundation
by Larson Publications
4936 State Route 414
Burdett, New York 14818 USA

99 98 97 96 95 94 93
10 9 8 7 6 5 4 3 2 1

COVER ART: *Narcissus* by a follower of Boltraffio, (late 15th century),
The National Gallery, London.

This translation is dedicated to the memory of J. N. T. G 1942-1965

CONTENTS

FOREWORD

 I hold her hands and press her to my breast.
I try to fill my arms with her loveliness, to
plunder her sweet smile with kisses, to
drink her dark glances with my eyes.

Ah, but where is it? Who can strain the blue
from the sky?
I try to grasp the beauty; it eludes me, leaving
only the body in my hands.
Baffled and weary I come back.
How can the body touch the flower which
only the spirit may touch?

—Rabindranath Tagore

Tagore had glimpsed his soul "out there" and been left to discover its trail. Louis Lavelle is exquisitely intimate with this
kind of moment—whether it comes through love, work, art,
music, religion, or a transparent mundane event like the one
Rupert Brooke immortalized in "Dining Room Tea." Lavelle's
profound understanding of our fascination with and resistance
to the power of such moments is what gives this superb book its
extraordinary value.

As we read, it becomes obvious that Narcissus—the beautiful but tragic youth of myth—does indeed live and die again in
each of us. He operates at many levels in every self-reflective
person. But he is most problematic for those who have

glimpsed their soul and known the deep melancholy that can settle in when that precious moment seems irretrievable.

It's no longer news that we each have something of extraordinary beauty within us. Americans have even elected a new president who insists that the only country worth having is one that will give that core of each of us a better chance to live. Thankfully, Lavelle neither flaunts his own nor seeks to gain our good opinion by flattering us about ours. Instead, he sets about explaining why it consistently eludes us, and how we might have better luck making it more than just a tantalizing dream.

A brief refresher in the myth of Narcissus will help us appreciate how he does it.

~

Even as a child, Narcissus was extraordinarily beautiful. A seer told his mother, "He will live to a ripe old age, provided that he never tries to know himself." From his very beginning, people of both sexes fell in love with him, longing to be an essential part of his life, longing for him to be an essential part of theirs. But Narcissus would have none of them.

Even Echo, the fairest of the nymphs, fell in love with him. But Narcissus spurned her also, vowing that he would rather die than let her loveliness have power over him. By the time he was sixteen, his path was strewn with spurned lovers.

There are at least two currently popular versions of what happens next.

In Robert Graves' version, a male suitor kills himself on Narcissus' threshold and calls on the gods for revenge. Artemis, the goddess of the woods and wild creatures, hears this plea. (The spurned Echo was still one of Artemis' favorites.) Artemis responds by making Narcissus fall in love, with the intention of denying him love's consummation.

In Edith Hamilton's version, a wounded lover prays: "May

he who loves not others love himself." This prayer is answered by the great goddess Nemesis, whose name means righteous anger.

Both versions are significant for different aspects of Lavelle's exposition, and both agree on the next turn of events. A thirsty Narcissus bends to take a drink. In Graves' version, the water is a spring, clear as silver, never yet disturbed by cattle, birds, beasts, or even the branches of the trees that shade it. In Hamilton's, it is simply a clear pool. In both versions, Narcissus sees and instantly falls in love with his own reflection. In both he is so enraptured by this image that he cannot leave it; but when he reaches out to it, he cannot grasp it either. He suffers the torment of seeming to possess, but not actually possessing, the beauty with which he longs to consummate.

In Graves' version, though grief torments him, Narcissus rejoices in his torment, knowing at least that this other self will be true to him whatever happens. Echo, who has not forgiven him but is still in love with him, joins in his grief. Finally, he cries to his reflection, "Ah, youth, beloved in vain, farewell" and plunges a dagger into his heart.

In Hamilton's version, Narcissus comes to the realization: "Now I know what others have suffered from me, for I burn with love of my own self—and yet how can I reach that loveliness mirrored in the water? But I cannot leave it. Only death can set me free." Here he doesn't kill himself violently but simply pines away, unable either to leave or to sustain himself through the image that entrances him.

In both versions, a new and exquisite flower blooms in the place where his body had expired, and it is given his name.

~

Many of us have paid dearly for confusing the self-preoccupied ego with that in us which is actually capable and worthy of love. Maybe we're fed up with the way Narcissus gets us so caught up in appearances and agendas that we lose touch with the invisible reality that sustains us. Or so caught up in our thoughts that our best impulses have no chance to live, no chance to express or inspire nobility of soul in our daily life. Maybe he can no longer fool us into thinking that the immaterial essence, the pure potentiality that we are, could ever be a fully accomplished thing—something to grasp as we grasp bodies. Maybe we're ready for a fresh look at the interdependence of the human family, rooted in a more inspiring vision than the economic/material model that is so often a ruse for exploitation. Maybe we've had enough of being punished along with Narcissus for trying to cheat life.

As even a brief glance at the table of contents of this book shows, what Lavelle offers here is much too rich to summarize briefly. But there are a few key things worth mentioning early on. He reminds us, for example, that "the whole art of living consists in preventing our intermittent good impulses from going to waste and withering away." He would help us take hold of them, set them to work, and make them bear fruit—but without spoiling them by thinking of ourselves as models for others as we do so.

Each of us is seeking a passion worthy of filling our soul to capacity. Without such a passion life is joyless, deprived of any light or goal worthy of the name. Seizing upon it means penetrating beneath all the superficial layers of consciousness, the domain of fleeting impressions, and into that mysterious region where those deep desires we acknowledge as our own are born. These, for Lavelle, are "our life's contact with the absolute." These are the things we took birth to realize, and the passion to realize them is the engine of what genius we have. For Lavelle, the essential sin—perhaps the only sin—is neglecting these deep impulses, this "fire which has been put in our keeping, and which it is for us to tend."

Discovering this "genius" in ourselves is where all the difficulty lies. For the most part, "we envy other people's, seeking to rival them instead of exploiting our own resources. Yet it cannot be denied that whenever we are faithful to ourselves, we experience a joy and a certitude which excel all other pleasures."

If we seek to analyze this genius, it vanishes. Often we can't help even doubting its very existence, as much of our life slips by in futility or tedium, dissipated by distractions. The very idea of a genius that is our very own stimulates what Lavelle calls *amour-propre*, which W.T. Gairdner has translated here as "self-love." Helping us through the dilemma that ensues is the purpose of this book.

Lavelle would have us see that "our genius is at the very opposite pole of our self-love, which consists of preoccupation with ourselves. . . . So far from supporting our genius, it obstructs its free operation." In fact, it is the very act of renouncing this self-love that reveals our genius to us.

To follow Lavelle, we must be willing to consider three things: first, the authentic integrity that is our genius must first be glimpsed inwardly; second, we must see that what we have glimpsed is a potential, not a fully actualized thing; and third, that this genius can complete itself only through relationships that keep us ahead of any self-image we can form.

In the process, Lavelle will introduce us to what he calls "the blessed paradox": the very point at which we are most ourselves is also the only point at which we are truly open to others; and none of us can realize our self except by co-operating in the realization of everyone else. One consequence is that each of us draws closer to others to the exact extent that we are faithful to ourselves. We cannot know one another so long as we try to act the part of spectator, casting an ineffectual eye on a finished product; we know one another only to the extent that we associate in a mutually life-giving stream, based in respect for the genius making itself in each of us. The impact of this idea on our notion of what true com-passion might be is enormous.

Maybe we're hungrier now for some of these ideas than the general public was when this book first appeared in French in

1939. Or when it first came into English in 1973. Maybe we're less inclined to desire those things which have become common through the universality of egoism, over those which can become common only when egoism is transcended.

Giving Lavelle a few chapters to hit his stride—for his themes to interweave and start to take flight—yields a series of liberating psychological insights, and something more. It also gives a fresh and invigorating look at a key philosophical point Plotinus thought so important to affirm seventeen centuries ago: our soul is not essentially self-knowing; its knowledge and existence come only as an active and subtly sensitive participation in the inner reality of the evolving world; we do it this way because we can't do it any other way. But if we take things and events at their face value, rather than for their inner significance, Narcissus' dilemma is our own.

The present point in space and the present moment in time, Lavelle reminds us, conceal sublime potentialities which raise small things above space and time. Here, where intelligence and body coincide, we win through to the awareness and possession of what we are—something not so much for us to know as to *realize*.

Larson Publications is delighted to reissue this book as the fourth in our series of classic reprints—books from the past that still outshine most others in their field.

PAUL CASH, DIRECTOR
January 1993

INTRODUCTION
Louis Lavelle (1883–1951)

1 *The Philosophy of Participation*

The life of Louis Lavelle was one with his thought. The latter began, he tells us,[1] with an intuition—dating from his earliest years, and never failing thereafter to excite in him delight and wonder—of the reality of his own free initiative, an initiative which was manifested every time he performed the most insignificant act, such as raising his little finger. This intuition contained, further, the realization that his own existence, at once separate from the world and independent of the law of cause and effect which reigns there, was also part of the world, since it could operate in it, and, by means of his body, effect changes in it. Indeed, his existence could only be realized by an act *in* the space-time world, an act which eternally modified that world.

In due course he reached the conviction that, just as he transcended the space-time world and yet possessed a body which was an object in that world, so his free initiative was at once independent of, and inhered in, the Pure Act, from which he must derive the very possibility of acting, and so of being. And this inherence of a finite will in an infinite will, this continuity of the finite and the infinite, led him on to the idea of *participation* as the link between the two, which is the distinctive theme of Lavelle's philosophy. Man is free, and he creates himself by exercising his freedom. And yet his freedom is not absolute; it can only be realized by an act of personal initiative, the "insertion' of himself into the Pure Act in which he inheres, and from which he derives not only his nature with its potentialities and its limitations, but also the very possibility of exercising his freedom, and so of creating himself.[2]

By placing the will and the fact of man's freedom at the center of his thought, Lavelle took his place, several years before J.-P. Sartre had published anything, in the Existentialist stream of modern philosophy (though in fact he consistently shuns the words *existential* and *existentialist*). But whereas Sartre deduces the absurdity of the idea of God and so the impossibility of His existence, Lavelle is *aware* of His existence from the start. For his intuition of his initiative as finite and limited implies and contains an intuition of an Infinite and Unlimited Initiative. The two are different aspects of the same intuition. From the first Lavelle is at an infinite distance from Sartre's "nausea"; his awareness of his own being, of the Pure Act in which he inheres, and of the world of other people and objects in and through which he acts, all this fills him with *joy*. For Lavelle, God is not to be thought of as an inaccessible goal to which we stretch out longing hands, but as the source of our being, of which we are aware in our awareness of ourselves.

Most of this came, perhaps, later. Meanwhile, having finished his graduate studies, and before he had completed his doctorate, the First World War broke out. Lavelle was called up, and in one of the engagements on the Western Front he was taken prisoner, and confined in a prisoner-of-war camp until the armistice. Here he achieved a feat which must surely be unique in the annals of university life. Without a single book, with nothing but a pen and a supply of paper, he composed his doctoral thesis, subsequently presented before the University of Strassbourg, and published with the title *La Dialectique du Monde Sensible*.[3] In this, his first work, he elaborates the implications of his conviction that the sensible world is composed of mere appearances, but is nevertheless a world which is significant for me, inasmuch as through the mediation of these appearances I can participate with the Pure Act in which I inhere, and also achieve communion with my fellow-men. For Lavelle, therefore, the world as we know it is our second link with the absolute.

Back from the war, Lavelle settled down to a life of teaching and writing, and in particular to the elaboration of his principal philosophical work, the four-volume *Dialectique de l'Éternal Présent*,[4] which became, as it developed, a splendid edifice, incorporating all the elements of his thought in its complex but integrated unity. It is planned as follows:

I *On Being*, 1928—the ideas and implications contained in the idea of being, finite and infinite.

II *On the Act*, 1934—Pure Act and finite act, and participation, their link; the finite self giving itself being by "inserting itself' into the Pure Act.

III *On Time and Eternity*, 1945—Time is a product of the perceiving mind and the form in which we make contact with reality; but we ourselves transcend time. An act can only be performed in the present, the past and future being real only as thoughts in our mind; reality is, therefore an eternal present. Only my body is subject to the law of time, and life in time is a process of converting matter to spirit. For things, together with events in time, pass away, but spirit is timeless; and yet things and events are important, since it is through them that I give myself being. It follows that time is in the present (the "Eternal Present") rather than the present in time; and time is a manifestation of Eternity, which is not a prolongation of time, but an eternal *present*. Life is a continual passing away, "the final death of the body being, not the end of life, but a moment of life, namely the moment at which the body is changed into spirit; and this is the work of consciousness, which is only possible if it is not time that contains consciousness, but consciousness which engenders time."[5]

IV *On the Soul*, 1951—a development of arguments of the three preceding volumes, showing how the individual liberty "inserts itself" into Pure Being through the instrumentality of its given nature, other people, and things.[6]

In 1941 Bergson died, and Lavelle was nominated as his successor in the Collège de France. Freed now from the routine teaching duties of a university professor, he could devote his life to reading, writing, and to the direction of the philosophical series called *La Philosophie de l'Esprit*[7] which he had founded with his friend René Le Senne in 1936. By the time of his death in 1951, some fifty philosophical works, French and foreign, contemporary and reprints, had appeared, the only link between the various authors being a common conviction, in opposition to the prevailing materialism, that ultimate reality is spiritual.[8]

2 The Œuvres Morales

Lavelle had intended to complete the four volumes of his *Dialectique de l'Éternel Présent* with a fifth, which was to be entitled *On Wisdom*, in which, we may presume, he would have discussed the practical problems of "participation' and the conditions to be fulfilled if it is to be realized. His death intervened before he had written more than a few pages of the plan. However, all through his active career he had interspersed his major works with shorter essays of a more concrete and practical nature—his *Œuvres Morales* as he calls them—and these give us, we may be reasonably certain, an impression of what *On Wisdom* would have been. They are, however, addressed to a wider public than the major works, and, while constantly restating his basic hypotheses, he does not attempt here to demonstrate them afresh, making them rather his point of departure.

The *Œuvres Morales* are these:

1933   *La Conscience de Soi* (Grasset); reprinted 1946, 1953
1939   *L'Erreur de Narcisse* (Grasset) (of which this volume is a translation); reprinted four times by 1963
1940   *Le Mal et la Souffrance* (Plon)
1942   *La Parole et L'Écriture* (Artisan du Livre)
1948   *Les Puissances du Moi* (Flammarion)

1951 *Quatre Saints* (Albin Michel) (short studies of Saint
Francis, Saint Theresa, Saint John of the Cross, and
Saint Francis of Sales). Translated into English by Dor-
othy O'Sullivan, with the title *The Meaning of Holiness*
(London, 1954); translated also into German, Spanish
and Italian

1957 *Conduite à l'égard d'autrui* (Albin Michel)

These minor works take their place in the tradition of the
great French *moralistes*, in whom psychological analysis and
moral teaching make a harmonious combination.[9] But the classical *moralistes* rely exclusively, or at any rate mainly, on acute
observation. Even La Rochefoucauld, whose starting-point is
the idea that all men are governed by *amour-propre* and self-interest, frequently forgets his own principle, for many of the
Maximes in fact prove the contrary. Lavelle's minor works show
the advantage a moralist derives from basic metaphysical insights. In them intuition, observation and argument go hand in
hand, each refining and deepening the other, and combining in
a unity which none of the classical moralists aspired to or attained. It is here especially that one can see that, for Lavelle, philosophy and life were one. Though death frustrated the comple-
tion of his life's plan, his work in its totality remains a finished
monument.

At the end of Jean École's *La Metaphysique de l'Etre dans la
Philosophie de Louis Lavelle*, the most thorough analysis of the
philosopher's work yet to be published, the author refers to the
strength, the beauty, and the organic development of Lavelle's
thought, and he concludes as follows: "It may well be—and the
appearance of numerous contemporary philosophies of being
suggests that it will be so—that Louis Lavelle will not remain
forever a voice crying in the wilderness, but that one day his
importance will be recognized; for his work indisputably marks
a turning-point in the history of contemporary philosophy,
while its author deserves as much, or more, Bergson's comment

on Maine de Biran: 'the greatest metaphysician France has produced since Descartes and Malebranche'" (op. cit., p. 257).

BIBLIOGRAPHICAL NOTE

Jean École has compiled in the work listed below a full bibliog-
raphy of the works of Louis Lavelle, which includes all his published books and articles, as well as the critical studies of his
philosophy by other writers. In addition to numerous articles,
four full-length volumes on Lavelle's philosophy have been
published to date:

Gonzague True: *De J.-P. Sartre à Louis Lavelle, ou Désagré-
gation et Réintegration*, Paris, Tissot, 1946

Jean École: *La métaphysique de l'être dans la philosophie
de Louis Lavelle*, Louvain, Éditions E.
Nauwelaerts, 1957

Wesley Piersol: *La valeur dans la philosophie de Louis Lavelle*,
Éditions Emanuel Vitte, 1959

Paule Levert: *L'être et le réel selon Louis Lavelle*, Paris,
Aubier, Éditions Montaigne, 1960

A doctoral thesis by a member of the faculty of the Université
du Québec à Trois-Rivières is also in preparation, with the title:
L'ideé de la liberté dans la philosophie de Louis Lavelle.

NOTE ON THE TRANSLATION

Two words in particular have caused difficulty:

1. *amour-propre.* The old meaning was "self-love," but the
word, both in modern French and as used by ourselves, means,
rather, a high opinion of oneself and of one's importance. I have
translated it as "self-love" whenever it seemed to me the context
definitely called for it; in all doubtful cases I have used the
French expression itself, leaving the reader to choose the shade
of meaning he feels appropriate.

2. *intimité.* "Intimacy" suggests a personal relationship,

which is not the sense in which Lavelle most often uses the word. But by *intimité* he means my inner being—which for him is the act accomplished in solitude by which I come to be, or give myself being. It is a form of consciousness or awareness, but one that cannot be communicated. *Intériorité* is another word he uses frequently; it has approximately the same meaning.

In preparing this translation, I have had the good fortune to enjoy the generous help of my colleague Dr. Carol Harvey, Ph.D. (Edin.), whose understanding of both the problems of translation and the world of existentialist thought has been of incalculable value.

All the footnotes and chapter prefaces are my own.

W.T. GAIRDNER
Department of French
University of Winnipeg
Canada 1973

Notes

1. In *Témoignage,* his last published article, and a condensed spiritual autobiography republished posthumously in the volume *Intimité Spirituelle* (Aubier, 1955).

2. Lavelle has often been accused by his opponents of pantheism, a strange charge, it would seem, to level against a thinker whose philosophy begins, continues and ends with his intuitive awareness of his individual initiative and liberty.

3. Lavelle re-edited this work, with only minor modifications, shortly before his death in 1951—a testimony to the unity of his thought, from the original intuition in which it began, through its complex elaboration, to its final summing-up and confirmation in *Témoignage.* In the camp in Germany, he also wrote the minor thesis required for the doctorate; this also was published after the war

with the title: *Perception visuelle de la profondeur* (publications de l'Université de Strasbourg, 1921, 72 pp.).

4. Aubier, Éditions Montaigne

5. These are actually the last words of *Témoignage* (p. 285) and the very last words, that Lavelle sent to a publisher, a few months before he died, but they resume the conclusions he reached in *On Time and Eternity.*

6. One other book by Lavelle should be classified among his major works, the two-volume *Traité des Valeurs* (Presses Universitaires de France, Vol. I, 1951, Vol. II, 1955).

7. Publ. Aubier.

8. There are statements scattered through *The Dilemma of Narcissus* (see especially Ch. IX) suggesting that Lavelle's work provoked bitter hostility in sections of the French public.

9. Readers of La Rochefoucauld will spot here and there sentences which might have come out of the *Maximes.* A good example is the first sentence of Ch. VIII of *The Dilemma of Narcissus.*

CHAPTER I

 LAVELLE uses three ancient myths to highlight the related problems of being and communication.

Narcissus has fallen in love with an image which he takes to be himself, though it is nothing but a *reflection* of himself, an *appearance*. He would know himself more completely, and he grasps at his reflection in the water. It eludes him, his real self being elsewhere, and unknowable. The appearance he sees reflects what he was, but what he has ceased to be.

To be, one must act, that is, go out from oneself in thought, action, or love. A narcissist (for Freud also made use of the myth) accepts this, and would make himself his own object. But this is impossible, for what he sees and loves is a mere image or appearance; it resembles him but is not him; yet on this appearance he allows his love to become fixed.

Since the image in the water cannot react to his love (nor Echo either, for she too is a mere reflection of himself), Narcissus finds himself alone. And not only alone, but withering away; for creative action demands, in addition to a free spirit, materials for this spirit to act upon; it is out of their opposition-and-cooperation that the act is born. Frustration leads Narcissus to exhaustion, and finally to death.

Pygmalion has fallen in love with a creation of his own imagination. Though the imagination, and especially that of the artist,[1] is indeed creative and of profound significance, its power is not that of the individual creating himself by the continuous operation of his will. The problem of communication, which for Lavelle is the major problem both of philosophy and life, can only be resolved between two autonomous individuals who have previously given themselves being.

Adam lives, because he goes out from himself in love for Eve, a real being and separate from him, who, like him, has given herself being by going out from herself in love for him. Eve breaks through her solitude when she sees her existence mirrored in Adam, this existence being however nothing more than a potentiality until a free soul has consented to it and willed it, taking possession of it and making it his own. Adam and Eve, having found themselves in each other, can now create, with a creativity that transcends that of the mere artist. The problem of communication is solved for them, and with it, the problem of life itself and its ultimate value.

The Dilemma of Narcissus

❧

1 *The legend*

The story of Narcissus has inspired the poets since Ovid.

Narcissus is sixteen years old. He is impervious to sensual desire. But the desire he has rejected will be transformed into a desire of a subtler kind.

His heart is pure. Since the contemplation of his own beauty might tempt him with sinful thoughts, it has been predicted that he will live a long life provided he does not try to know himself; but Destiny has decided otherwise. The innocent young man, being thirsty, goes off to a virgin spring, where no one's image has ever yet been reflected. In the water he suddenly sees his beautiful body, and now his thirst is for himself and for himself alone. His own beauty has become a tormenting longing, which separates him from himself by showing him his image, and which drives him to seek himself where alone he sees himself—namely, where he has ceased to be.

He sees before him an object which resembles him, which accompanied him to this spot, and which follows him at every step. "I smile at you," he says, "and you smile at me. To you I hold out my arms, and you stretch out yours to me. It is clear that you, too, are imploring me to clasp you to myself. If I weep because I know that this is impossible, you weep with me, and the tears, which bind us together in the common consciousness of our desire and our separation, blur the water's transparency, and suddenly hide us from one another."

Then, like a fencer, he begins a series of manoeuvres, of feints and passes: again and again he steps back from himself in order to see himself, and then leaps forward to clutch himself. He has had to go out from himself in order to give himself someone to love, and yet the object of his passion would dissolve away if he succeeded in reaching it. Nothing but a little water separates him from himself. He thrusts his arms in to grasp what he longs for, but which must remain forever a mere image. He can gaze at himself, but he cannot lay hold upon himself. He is wasting away, but he cannot tear himself from the spot. And now there lives on at the bring of the stream a memorial to his pitiful fate, a flower, with white petals and a saffron-colored heart.

2 *The nymph Echo*

Narcissus is expecting that his eyes, his eyes alone, will reveal his essential self, and the tragedy is that what he sees with his eyes is nothing more than its appearance.

He is mute; he has no desire to hear himself. All he asks is to see himself; to seize his beautiful, silent body as though it were a prey—this body which, if it uttered words, would thereby assume some sort of initiative; his desire might then be inhibited, and his possessing become a mutual exchange.

However, his failure finally impels him to call to the image, and to implore it to reply. The solitude which is his present lot and which he had hoped to end, is beginning to frighten him. He is willing, now, to break the unity of this absolute silence and, as he gazes into the depths of the pool, to seek signs of an independent life within this form—a form which resembles his own but which, in reality, is nothing more than his reflection.

But the echo sends him back his own voice, as though to convince him that he is still alone, and his solitude becomes deeper still. This reply, which imitates his words and is nothing but a mockery of a response, finally separates him from himself, carrying him off to a world of illusion, where his own existence melts away and eludes him altogether.

Narcissus' punishment is this: no one loves him except the

nymph Echo. He is seeking in the pool another being to love him, and finds none. He cannot escape from himself. No other love but his love of himself pursues him; but *this* love is ever at his heels, even at those very moments when he tries hardest to detach himself from it.

According to the myth, young Narcissus cannot be separated from the nymph Echo, who is his awareness of himself. Echo loves Narcissus, but she may not speak first to tell him of her love, for she has no voice of her own. She repeats what Narcissus says, but only some of his words. "Is there anyone near me?" says Narcissus. "Me," Echo repeats. And when Narcissus says: "Let us meet together," Echo repeats: "together."[2] Everlastingly she sends him back his own words, ironically mutilated. She never answers them.

3 *Pool or spring*

The pool which could send back to Narcissus a faithful and fully-formed image of himself does not exist. This one is a spring; in it, moment by moment, Narcissus himself comes to life, but the water never ceases to bubble up, coruscating its surface, and refusing him an image with a clearly defined outline. Now let us suppose that for the fraction of a second the spring should cease to flow, that the surface of the water should become motionless and smooth like a real mirror—will he be able to contemplate himself at last, as though held fast in frozen transparency? No; once again, he would be doomed to disappointment. For this mirror would be so sensitive that his very breathing would be sufficient to cloud it. Should he draw nearer, his breath, like a gentle breeze, would set a host of ripples racing across its surface, which he could in no way still.

His pathetic enterprise is doomed in advance, for it is self-contradictory. Narcissus is trying to remain himself—an invisible liberty, a thought, a possibility, a pure sentiment as yet unavowed—and at the same time to catch a glimpse of himself as an object on which he might stay his gaze, as a landscape unfolding before him, as a face—an upturned face. He is trying to become the spectator of himself, a spectator of the inner act through which he is at every moment being reborn, an act which, were it ever to, become a visible object, would straight-way cease to be. He watches himself, instead of living; and this is his first sin. He tries to find his essence, and finds nothing but his image, which leaves him eternally dissatisfied.

All that he sees of himself is the reflection of his body, beauti-ful, and still pure. But in the end the spectacle unnerves him: from now onwards, he loses his capacity to live.

4 *The silvering of the mirror*

The mirror in which Narcissus gazes would be ineffective if it were pure transparency, but it is silvered. What, then, is the silvering?

Narcissus conceals within himself the infinite depth of being and life. And his face is reflected at the precise point at which he halts his descent into himself—this self which has no final limit. He is looking for his soul in the mirror: *amour-propre* and his de-sire to possess himself constitute the mirror's silvering; they set a limit to his pursuit of himself, and at the same time offer him the image of his body. It is true that his excitement on discover-ing himself is the excitement of having discovered the absolute in which he participates. But this can bring him no satisfaction; as yet he has found no place and no object where his longing may come to rest.

Imagine Narcissus before the mirror. The glass and its silver-ing constitute a barrier blocking his further progress. His face strikes against them; he batters them with clenched fists; if he goes behind them there is nothing there. The mirror holds pris-oner within itself a dimension which eludes him, a world in which he sees himself but cannot lay hold of himself, and from which he is separated by an impression of space which he can diminish to any extent, but never abolish.

Yet all the while the pool is beckoning to him, like a road stretching away into the distance. Before ever meeting his image, he delighted in the transparency of the water and its perfect purity, as yet unsullied by any contact. But perfect lucidity did not satisfy him, he passes through it in search of his image, as soon as it has taken shape. And now the world which beckoned him holds him eternally prisoner: the moment he enters it his doom is sealed.

5 *The past and death*

I cannot see myself in any other way than by turning round and contemplating my past, but that is to contemplate something I have already ceased to be. To live is to create my own being by turning my will towards a future in which I do not yet exist, and which will not become an object which can be contemplated until I have not only reached it, but have gone beyond it.

Now the consciousness of self which Narcissus is seeking destroys his will to live, which is to act. For in order to act, he must cease watching himself and thinking about himself; he must refuse to transform a spring, whose water should purify, nourish, and strengthen him, into a stagnant pool.

But he is enamored of his body, which will disintegrate one day, and of his past, which he pursues as it slips away into the shadows. He is like a man writing his memoirs, and savoring his own history, before the end has come. Looking in a mirror is like watching your past advancing towards you, for only by looking backward can one read in a mirror the secret of one's destiny.

And so Narcissus is punished for cheating, for he wishes to contemplate his being before he has himself created it. He seeks in himself, and attempts to grasp, an existence which is in fact nothing but a pure potentiality, just in so far as it has not yet been exercised. Narcissus stops at this potentiality; he turns it into a deceptive image; it is here that he takes up his abode rather than in his real being. He has made the most fatal error he could make, namely to imagine that by creating this seductive image of himself he has created his true being.

It is only as a man advances in life that he begins to be capable of seeing himself. Then he may turn round, take stock of the ground covered, and observe the tracks his feet have left. The spring in which Narcissus gazes should not be visited before nightfall. One day, he may see in it a shadowy form, but only as he approaches his decline—at the moment when he himself is about to become a shadow. It is then that his being and his image draw together, and finally merge. But young Narcissus came to gaze in the spring at dawn; he tried to glimpse what was not given to him to see, and it was his tragic destiny to deliver up his body to the image in which he had thought to grasp it.

All he can do now is to identify himself with this lifeless lay-figure. He is condemned to a premature and needless death, because he has grasped at a privilege which he has done nothing to deserve—a privilege which death alone can bestow upon a man—that of beholding, as he looks upon himself, his own creation, when, and only when this creation is complete.

6 *A stranger who is himself*

No one can see himself completely in the lay figure which reflection presents. It is himself, and not himself. After his most strenuous efforts to be two people, Narcissus encounters an inverted and complementary image of himself—a mere mirror-image. His soul is the permanent dialogue between the self and its image which, in fact, constitutes the alternations of our awareness of life. He seeks, but he cannot realize, the exact coincidence of the two—a coincidence which would abolish them both.

And so we see ourselves as another person; and this other

person is not someone else; what we see is nothing more than a reflection of ourselves—and one that the hand cannot seize, or the mirror preserve, a false image, an unfaithful reproduction.

Narcissus is so close to himself that he draws away from himself to get a better view; but now he cannot get back to himself. And in the spring he sees a face which never changes, and yet the face seems always new, because it is forever the same stranger, the same person who remains forever unknown. Narcissus is hoping for a miracle: the conversion of his being into something he will be able to see as another sees him. And it is his desire to love himself as another might love him that drives him to try to know the image of himself which others see. But others see this image as alive, while he has drained life out of it.

It is at this point that the drama begins: for the image of himself lacks even the consistency of the most fragile object; unlike a mirage which only deceives if it is far away, it stays so close to him that, if he draws away ever so little, it melts to nothing. Narcissus is attempting the impossible, for he will never realize a true separation from this image, nor will he ever exactly coincide with it, nor again will he ever achieve that interaction between activity and passivity which is the mark of every true action.

Narcissus is excited by the sensation of his own existence. As he observes himself, he produces an image of himself that resembles the images of other people which, until then, had held his attention. He reproduces this image over and over again, by making movements of which he is both the spectator and the author. He begins to believe in a mutual attraction. But this image which he is gazing at in the stream, this image, too, is stretching out its arms to another, and not to him.

Narcissus is becoming estranged from himself; it is as though he were looking at himself from outside; and suddenly he appears to himself as indeed a stranger, and one he cannot understand. He is like a lunatic, running away from himself and then pursuing the fleeing image; and his end is like Ophelia's. Since he is alive, what need has he of this image of his life, an image which is meant for others and not for him?

7 *The shadow of a shadow*

If it were really true that Narcissus had become two people, he would find a fragment of himself in his double. But instead of dividing his essential self, he makes an image of it, his real self remaining forever invisible; and what he makes visible is nothing but a shadow, empty and unreal.

Narcissus needs to be reassured about his own existence, the reality of which he doubts, which is why he tries to catch sight of it. But he must resign himself to being able to see the world and not being able to see himself. For how could he, the seer, see himself, except by transforming himself into the object seen, from which his real self is absent? He who can throw his arms about any object he pleases, how could he throw his arms about himself? He must go forth from himself if he is to possess himself; if he seeks himself, he will waste away in the search.

He who is the origin of every presence, and who endows with presence everything that exists, how could he become present to himself?

The man who knows a thing cannot possess the existence of what he knows. But Narcissus is trying to combine being and knowing in the same mental act. He does not realize that he only comes to be in and through his knowledge of the world. He interrupts his life in order to know it, only to find that he is now confronted by an image from which life itself has departed. He is nothing but an empty vessel, the shape of which becomes visible only because of the presence of the liquid it contains.

Narcissus knows nothing of this spring in which he admires himself, of the green leaves in which he is hiding, of the immense world around him; all that he recognizes is this fragile reflection of himself which takes shape in the bosom of these things, and which, were it not for them, would not exist.

9 *The sin against the spirit*
Narcissus is secretive and lonely.

His delusion is a subtle one. He is a spirit who tries to watch himself as though he were a character in a play. He commits the sin against the spirit, which consists in trying to grasp himself in the same way as he grasps bodies; but this he cannot do, and it is his body which he destroys the moment he shatters its reflection. The image entices him, fascinates him; it draws him away from all real objects; in the end, he has no eyes for anything else. In order to enjoy himself, he makes an idol of himself, so that the object of his delectation may ever be at hand. But it is only a dreamer who can thus produce an image of himself; and this image perishes with his dream.

And the tragedy of Narcissus is that the spring was the true source of the lay-figure he is contemplating; he did not create it. It was a reflection in the spring which enabled him to recognize himself. However, an image presupposes a being who is reflected, and this being has ceased to interest him. So it is that he loses the more precious thing that he had, while the less precious thing that he desired in exchange is refused him. And yet, the humblest act would suffice to deliver him from his wretchedness, and restore the being which he has lost. This is the lesson to be learned from his sad story—a story re-enacted eternally down the ages of man.

10 *Death or Birth?*
Must we conclude that Narcissus dies of grief on seeing a beauty which is his, but which must ever remain for him a mere spectacle? The image which he would grasp is more beautiful than himself, but it is elusive and inviolable, like all shadows and all reflections.

Or shall we rather conclude that his grief comes from the discovery, by means of the image, that he has a material form—he who thought that he was pure spirit? And must we believe the

myth, according to which Narcissus' youthful death is indeed
the concluding scene of his sorry drama? It is possible to inter-
pret the story otherwise. From this death Hermes brings forth a
new life, which illustrates the fact that the two opposites, Death
and Life, are inseparable. When man saw the reflection of his
form in water or his shadow on earth, and saw that it was beautiful, he fell in love with it and sought to possess it. His desire
made him the prisoner of this form. The form seizes her lover,
winds herself about him, and they are united in a mutual passion. Such (according to this version of the legend) is the story of
the incarnation of Narcissus, and how he began his mortal existence.

11 *Narcissus and Pygmalion*

Imagination seems to breathe life into everything it creates.
There is a dreamer in every man, a dreamer who can say: "On a
certain day in my life, I called up before my eyes the image of
Alexander, and little by little I watched it come alive before me.
Soon the young man began to move and to give all the signs of
life and of presence. He had the face of an adolescent, slightly
tilted to one side as the chroniclers relate, rounded but not
fleshy, the features as yet incompletely formed, calm, beautiful,
a trifle wayward." But the dream fades at the instant of its birth.

Ever and anon, each of us thinks he can give life to an image
by willing it. For a moment he is intoxicated by his own power,
but he ends in despair. The act of creation eternally rejoices the
heart of God only because, in creation, He calls to life a real being, endowed with a body, a soul, and the capacity for free initiative, a being who can call upon Him, and respond to Him.
Whereas our imaginings leave us with ourselves.

There is a tragic similarity between Narcissus' destiny and
Pygmalion's. Pygmalion has never loved a woman. One day,
while contemplating the statue he has made, he finds it irresist-
ibly beautiful. The work of his hands begins to excite his passion at the very moment he should be separating from it. He

calls upon Venus, and his unvoiced supplication seems to soften the ivory and turn it into flesh. The motionless body is all the more seductive because, as it seems to him, it refuses to respond out of womanly modesty; Pygmalion shrinks from offending it. However he soon imagines that it is returning his caresses. And the ardor of his love is such that he thinks he can win a response through the sheer intensity of his desire, and that ultimately this inert object will be changed into the body of a woman. "My love," he thinks, "has miraculous powers." The contrary is true: it has all the characteristics of the passion of the helpless and rejected lover whose lust has changed the body of a woman into a mass of inert matter.

Pygmalion is in love with the work of his hands, but it can only frustrate him if it remains an object of his contemplation and his admiration. To cease to be its slave, he must break with it and forget it.

Narcissus sees nothing but his own image. Pygmalion does indeed borrow from the universe a little matter to endow it with a different form; but, contemplating a thing which he has made, he would change this thing into a living soul: he is so confident in the power of his love that he thinks himself capable of giving life to the object of his desires. Herein lies his impiety; for the only life he can love is one which must first give itself being, before it can give itself to him.

12 *Adam and Eve*

God, in His sovereign wisdom, saw Adam seeking himself, like Narcissus; and making of him two persons according to his desire, he presented before him the body of the woman to which he could be united without destroying himself. But Narcissus, abandoned to his own resources, duplicated himself with a phantom which could do nothing but imitate his pathetic gestures and, just when he thought himself about to grasp his true self, the image transformed this self into an illusion which drove him to despair.

Milton gives another version of the myth: he uses it princi-
pally to represent the awakening of self-consciousness, or the
relation of man to himself. These nascent potentialities can only
be realized if they are completed by a living relationship between the man and a woman, and between one individual and
every other. Narcissus feels this feminine principle within himself; but it mocks him, he cannot satisfy it. In Milton's myth, Eve
is born into the light, in the twinkling of an eye, and seeks to
know what she is, and whence she has come. Nature has taught
her nothing. She bends over the surface of the waters which reflect the purity of the sky, and which to her appear to be a second sky. As she leans over, she perceives a figure advancing towards her. "When I look at it," says Eve, "it looks at me. I start,
and draw back; it, too, starts, and draws back. Some secret spell
draws me to it; the same spell draws it towards me. Does not all
this suggest we were destined for each other?" But, entranced
though she is, Eve does not yield at once; she will not yet let her
eyes linger with desire upon Adam. A voice must first assure
her that her very existence is imaged there before her eyes.
"What you contemplate, beautiful creature," affirms the voice,
"is yourself." But to Eve it appears that what she sees, and what
is even now filling her with admiration, is another being. Never
for a moment was it the image of herself that she was pursuing
and seeking to possess. It was someone other than herself, and
yet she realizes, as she gazes at this other's image, that he is also
similar to herself. She will be united to him, and will give him,
says the poet, a multitude of children, who will call her the
mother of all living.[5]

Notes

1. Lavelle was extremely sensitive to the arts, and has some profound things to say about them. See for example *Les Puissances du Moi*, Book II.

2. The French original reads: *Et quand Narcisse dit: "Réunissons-nous," Echo redit: "Unissons-nous."* Narcissus wants communication and friendship, Echo offers union without either.

3. Spanish poet, 1561–1627.

4. In the Brentano version of the legend, the Lorelei stands on a rock above the Rhine, looking for an ideal lover; but such a being has no real existence, and in despair she throws herself into the water.

5. See *Paradise Lost*, IV: 449–491.

> *(Eve is speaking)*
>
>   . . . (I) laid me down
> On the green bank, to look into the clear
> Smooth Lake, that to me seemed another Sky.
> As I bent down to look, just opposite,
> A shape within the wat'ry gleam appear'd
> Bending to look on me, I started back,
> It started back, but pleased I soon return'd
> Pleas'd it return'd as soon with answering looks
> Of sympathy and love; there I had fixt
> Mine eye till now, and pin'd with vain desire,
> Had not a voice thus warn'd me, What thou seest,
> What there thou seest fair creature is thy self,
> And I will bring thee where no shadow staies
> Thy coming, and thy soft imbraces, he
> Whose image thou art, him thou shalt enjoy
> Inseparably thine, to him shalt bear
> Multitudes like thy self, and thence be call'd
> Mother of human Race . . .

(Eve still shrinks back, but finally yields to Adam after he has reassured her as follows:)

> Return fair *Eve*,
> Whom fli'st thou? whom thou fli'st, of him thou art,
> His flesh, his bone; to give thee being I lent
> Out of my side to thee, nearest my heart
> Substantial Life, to have thee by my side
> Henceforth an individual solace dear;
> Part of my Soul I seek thee, and thee claim
> My other half...

For Lavelle, Milton's account of the story of the creation of Eve from Adam's rib expresses the idea that we become wholly ourselves only through others, and notably through love, which is an act of self-giving.

CHAPTER II

INTIMACY, the secret place of my will where my act, and so myself, come to be. Now because every soul inheres in the Pure Act, each man's secret, while remaining inviolably his own, is also the secret of every other man. This discovery is both the confirmation and the end of one's solitude; it is my own self-creation stimulated by the other man's, and his by me; it is the meaning and the purpose of life; it is at once the road home and home itself.

Thus other people are indispensable to us for our self-knowledge and for our growth, in other words for our coming to be our real selves. These are truths Narcissus did not understand.

Our attitude to others and the judgements we pass on them are identical with our attitude to ourselves and the judgement we pass on ourselves.

because a judgement is a false image that is designed to stop my true revelation and movement towards a maturity.

The Secret of Intimacy

❧

1 *Know thyself*

Narcissus thinks he can find the secret of the world in himself, and that is why he fails to find himself. For this divine secret is closer to him than he is himself: it is the intimacy of pure Being. This has no image. It is not in the pool which is reflected in the mind of Narcissus and which returns to its original mystery the moment he turns his eyes away. It discloses itself to none but a purely spiritual apprehension, operating in a world beyond all images and all mirrors.

All that is most noble and most beautiful in the world that my imagination can conceive, all that for me bears value and is hence worthy of my love—all *that* is my deepest intimacy; and when I run away from it, excusing myself as unworthy or incapable, I run away from myself. The most superficial things or the basest, which beckon to me or hold me captive, are distractions drawing me away from myself; it is not so much that I cannot bear the sight of what I am, but that I lack the courage to exercise the powers I have at my disposal, or to satisfy the demands whose voice I hear within me.

We cannot discover that our being is to be found in this secret intimacy, wherein none penetrates but ourselves, without having recourse to introspection. But the self is nothing but a possibility waiting to be realized, and never completely made; it has never done making itself. That is why there are two introspections: one which is wholly bad, and which shows me all those passing states of myself over which I endlessly linger, and the other, which is wholly good, and which fixes my attention on an *activity* which is my very own, on the potentialities which I can awaken and which it is within my power to use, on values which I strive to discern so that I may body them forth.

For self-consciousness is not a light which illuminates a pre-existent reality without changing it, but an activity which deliberates on its decisions and holds its own destiny in its hands. "Know thyself," said Socrates, as though he had Narcissus already in mind. But Socrates was fully aware that the man who knows himself is also endlessly deepening himself and so transcending himself. If the Greeks of old repeat "Know thyself" and the Christians "Forget thyself," it is because they are not speaking of the same self: and I can only know the one on the condition that I forget the other.

2 *Intimacy with oneself and with others*

There is an inwardness[1] which no eye can see, but it is reality's ultimate bedrock, beyond which it is impossible to go, and which one cannot reach without first passing through all the superficial layers which vanity, easy conformism, or habit have wrapped around it. The root of things is at this point, every beginning and every birth; it is at once the source and the center, the purpose and the meaning.

Its discovery is difficult, and once found, it remains for us to make our own permanent abode; and yet it is here that we find the source of our strength and the cure of all our ills. It is because they have never been there that so many men run after distractions, or think to reform the world from without. But the man who has once found his way into this secret place[2] will never consent to be banished; the lure of pleasure and the enticement of surface action have vanished away.

It is indeed, as many believe, the remotest point of solitude. But also, the moment we discover it, we are no longer alone. A world opens out which is within us but into which every being can be invited. An apprehension may arise that perhaps we are

indeed still alone, and that this inner world is but a dream island. But should another enter with us, this dream becomes a
reality, and this island a continent. Then we know the keenest
joy the soul can know. It is revealed to us that our most secret
world, the world we thought so fragile, is common to all, the
only world which is not mere appearance, an absolute which is
present within us, but which is spread out before us, and in
which we are called to live.

It is individual and universal at one and the same time. The
intimacy which I suppose I have with myself is realized only in
the intimacy of my communication with another. Intimacy is always shared—the common use of the word confirms the fact. I
would remain separate from myself so long as I could not communicate what I am and, in the act of communicating it, discover it.

He who imparts his intimacy to another does not talk about
himself; what he communicates is a spiritual universe which is
within him and which is the same for all men. He enters it not
without a sort of trembling. Commonplace souls on the other
hand never get beyond the threshold, while those of the baser
sort avoid it and seek to bring it into disrepute; true being is
there and nowhere else, but all they feel is scorn and hatred.

3 *The secret which is common to all*

There is in each of us a secret essence, into which we scarcely
dare to direct our gaze; this, like the prying eye of a stranger,
would, we feel, lay it bare and violate our privacy. But the
miracle is that I suddenly find that my secret is also yours, and
that so far from being a dream without reality, it is reality itself
and the world is its dream; it is a silent voice, but the only one
that can awaken an echo. For the point where each man is alone
with himself is the same point where he truly opens himself to
others. And the mystery of the self, where it reaches the deepest
levels, where it is felt to be truly unique and inexpressible, produces a sort of excess of solitude, a solitude which then shatters,

because it is the same for all. And it is only then that I have the
right to use those admirable words: "I open my heart to you";
that is to say, I abolish all that has hitherto been secret in me,
and at the same time open my heart in welcome to what is secret
in you.

For it is only by another man that I can expect to be con-
firmed and made secure in a spiritual existence which, without
his presence, would remain subjective and illusory. Not that
when an exterior object is in question I need to call upon his
experience as if mine had been untrustworthy. We are not concerned here with a spectacle which is offered to all alike, on
which the eyes of all alike converge and meet. We are concerned
with that *invisible* reality from which I thought, once, that I drew
the nourishment of my most personal life, but which then
seemed fragile and unsubstantial, and which I scarcely dared to
assume so long as I looked upon it solely as mine. But now that
another reveals its presence in him also, it brings me a sort of
miraculous light; it assumes extraordinary density and definition; the visible world, which had previously given me such a
sense of security, retreats and becomes less substantial, like a
stage set.

4 *Solitude deepened and shattered*

In the cell of his self-consciousness the self is shut in as in a
prison. It is in distress because it cannot tear itself away from
itself, nor free itself from itself. It is forever alone; and yet it is
that which has the power to enter into communication with all
that is. It is this which makes it a spirit. But it alone can know
and it alone can exercise this capacity to communicate. Of this
power it is true to say that it can break the soul's solitude, and
that it can deepen it.

We should not linger over much about our consciousness of
self. This makes us restless, and excites desire; it converts being
and life itself into objects; the self-centered self then seeks to
possess these, and claims the right to enjoy them. But this is not

to go down to the very root of being and life. By means of this exclusive attention to itself, the self hopes to exalt itself; but in the end it wastes away. For the truth is rather that its very existence depends on the objects of its knowledge and its love. And so it is essential that the self leave itself in the quest both of knowledge and of love; in other words, in the quest of an opportunity to give itself that existence which it had first thought to seize out of hand. It is only then that it discovers the secret of knowledge, and the secret of love.

Sometimes solitude is a temptation; we lavish all our skill to maintain it and protect it. But the wise man sees in it no more than a sort of spiritual exercise which proves its value and creative power in those contacts with the world without which it had appeared originally to sever. Only thus we learn to live as we imagined life when we were alone. If we imagine, in our solitude, a life in perfect harmony with ourselves, with the universe, and with all men, it is our return to the world which, by a sort of paradox, gives reality to this solitude and enables it to bear fruit.

5 *Encounter*

Meeting with any man we find upon our way is inevitably accompanied by emotion, an ambiguous emotion where fear and hope mix. What is going on behind this face which resembles ours, a face which we can see, while we cannot see our own? Is he offering peace or war? Will he take possession of our living-space, reduce the scope of our activities, drive us from our little sphere and occupy it himself? Or will he, on the contrary, widen our horizon, extend our life, increase our strength, promote our wishes, establish with us that spiritual communion which will drag us out of our solitude, introduce a genuine interlocutor into the dialogue which we maintain with ourselves—one who is not the echo of our voice—and so bless us at last with a new and unimagined revelation?

We always feel this emotion in the presence of another man,

one whom we think we know and love the best, or indeed any and every man. He is not us, but he is, as we are, capable of enterprise, alive and free, able to think and to will, and whose least initiative, we feel, may transform our thoughts and feelings, and our very destiny. The history of our relationship with him is the history of this emotion which he continues to excite in us, of its fluctuations, and of the hopes it arouses, which the event will sometimes fulfill, sometimes disappoint. But it may happen that this emotion fades almost immediately, the mingled fear and hope disappear little by little; the man who passed close to us has become once more a passer-by of no more importance for us than the stones along the wayside. We have sent him back, alive, to the void from which our attention had for a moment drawn him. The concern, so rich in the inseparable but contrary possibilities which had been aroused by our first meeting, and which, at its inception, had raised questions in our minds on the outcome of the adventure, all this died no sooner than it began. We were trembling then, not knowing whether we should desire his presence or his absence, whether love or hatred was about to be born, whether his coming was to bring us blessings or distress. And we already had an inkling that if a close relationship were to develop, all these things, so far from excluding each other, would come to us together.

6 *Reciprocity*

It should come as no surprise that the deepest desire of our hearts, and the one which motivates our conduct, is to find other men with whom we would like to live, or, if we are more modest and less self-confident, with whom we could bear, merely, to live. For in our heart of hearts we feel that there is no other problem for a man than that of learning to live with other men. And all the miseries of life come from the fact that we cannot do this.

A sign, however discreet, that a rift has opened out between myself and another man, is sufficient to stifle all the movements of my heart, not only those which drew me towards him, but even those which composed, in the quiet of solitude, the spontaneous flow of my inner life. And the least sign of the rebirth of communion, involuntary perhaps, unconscious even, is enough to bring them to life once more, opening out before us the infinity of spiritual space.

But it often happens that this same presence of other men which we expected to become the occasion of the expansion of our liberty and a deep well-spring of joy—a presence which we had not merely accepted but desired and loved—inhibits us, leaves us forlorn, is almost more than we can bear. We should not forget, however, that when we begin a dialogue with ourselves similar to that which we have with the other man, we do not always find it easy to tolerate what we are. For in each of us there is an extremely exacting being, in whose eyes no man, not even ourselves, finds grace. But the essence of patience is learning to suffer, in ourselves and in others, the wretchedness of the individual self, and the essence of charity is to bring succor to the afflicted.

Most men, it is true, are harder on others than on themselves, and the essence of virtue would seem to consist in the reversal of the natural order. But we must not forget that the self within us is also a being who is other than ourselves, and that he who is ungentle with this other will never be gentle with anyone; and the worst of all would be if he pretended to be.

I am wrong, doubtless, if I complain of the treatment I receive from others, for it is always an effect and a reflection of the way I treat them. I am grieved because others do not love me enough, but the reason is my own lovelessness. It is the warmth of welcome which I bear within me which makes others warm to me, and they reject me only if, in the bottom of my heart, I have already rejected them. Now man is so made that he is not conscious of this reciprocity: he would be noticed by those he cares nothing for, and thought much of by those he despises. "But with what measure ye mete it shall be measured to you again."[3]

I have never done accusing others; I ignore them, loudly protesting that I despise them, that I have no desire to know them. But I cannot do without them. This contempt I feel for them is nothing but the sign of my need to esteem them; and it dictates my duty towards them, which is to give them enough love to make them worthy of my esteem.

7 *Self-knowledge and knowledge of others*

Being is always more than knowledge. For knowledge is a spectacle spread out before us. And for this reason there is nothing which is as completely unknown to us as the being which we are; we can never separate it from our image. In one sense it may be said that every man knows more about me than I do myself; but he is in no stronger position on that account. For one must not know too precisely what one is if one wishes to be wholly the person one is.

It is natural that I should know others better than myself, I who am busy making myself. And that is why there is so much vanity, dissembling, and waste of time in the persistence with which I contemplate myself. It holds me back when I should be acting. I must leave this preoccupation to others, who are not directly responsible for what I am to become, and who, unlike myself, are concerned with my realized being more than with the act which calls it into being. They see in me the man already revealed, he who differs from everyone else in his character and in his weaknesses, and not the man I want to be, he who is forever seeking to transcend his nature and cure his imperfections. I am vaguely aware of the presence in myself of a power as yet unused, a hope as yet not disappointed. Another, observing me, sees nothing but the being I can show him, whereas what I am conscious of is the being I can never show. Unlike him, my eyes are always fixed on what I am not rather than on what I am, my ideal rather than on my present state, on the goal of my desires rather than the distance by which I am separated from it.

Misunderstanding between men always arises from the different perspectives in which a man sees himself and others. For what he sees in himself is his potentialities, while in others, it is their actions. And the allowance he makes for himself he refuses to make for others. A kinship between them is born as soon as they begin to go beyond what they can show, evincing that mutual trust which is nothing else than silent co-operation.

But egoism blinds a man. Finding in myself a sentient, thinking, and active being, I see, nevertheless, in others, mere objects which can be described, or tools to be made use of. And so it should not surprise us that he who knows everything about himself does not know himself; and further, for opposite reasons, that everyone remains forever unknown both to himself and to others.

The most difficult thing in our relations with others is what may appear the simplest: namely to recognize in them that individual existence by which they resemble us and yet are different from us, that presence in them of a unique and irreplaceable individuality, of an initiative and a liberty, of a vocation which is their own and which we must help them to realize, instead of feeling jealous of it, or seeking to bend it in the hopes of making it serve ours. For us, this is the first command of charity, and perhaps also the last.

8 *The painter and the portrait*

Our eye, says Plato, can see itself in the pupil of another's eye.

It is others who reveal me to myself. I gradually become conscious of what I think and what I feel through the thoughts and the feelings which they force upon my attention. And their acts reflect back to me the image of what I am, whether these acts repeat mine or whether they are a reaction to them.

Inversely, to understand someone else is to discover in oneself all the impulses one observes in him; it is to abandon oneself to them for a moment, so much so that just when one thinks one is following them, it is oneself that one is following. It may even happen that one anticipates his impulses.

People cannot know themselves apart, but only by means of a mutual comparison which brings out their similarities and their differences. This comparison which allows each of us to discover and try out his own potentialities, is not without its dangers. For it may incline us to be satisfied with mere imitation, when the self, thinking to enrich itself, fades away into an unreal sham; or else it may induce a habit of systematic disparagement, by which we think to raise ourselves up by dint of denigrating everything we lack. And yet every contact we make shows us, by the resistances which it provokes, by the effort which it demands of us, by the light which it creates, by a feeling, suddenly born in us, of the coming of a secret understanding, how intermingled and inseparable are self-knowledge and the knowledge of others.

This is clear in the case of an artist painting a self-portrait. When a painter paints himself, he paints the portrait of another man; and his portrait of another man is a self-portrait too. For he cannot paint anything except what he is not—what is different from him and contrary to him. And so, when he paints himself, he forces himself to discover the face which others see when they look at him. But when he paints someone else he creates a work of art which comes from within him, and which lays bare before the world what otherwise would remain forever invisible, namely his own invisible vision of the world. To know myself is at one and the same time to make another person of myself and to confront myself with another person. To know you I must become so deeply aware of myself that I find myself in you: in you I see this outward manifestation of an act, whereas introspection gives me only the inner experience of performing it.

And so it is that what I find in another is never anything else than a reflection of myself. Its features are sometimes inverted and complementary to mine; they may be more clearly marked, or they may be vaguer. But they are meaningless unless I experience in myself this same life to which they give a form. All men are continually sending back and forth to each other an image of themselves, an image which is both true and false, and even when utterly alone my interlocutor is a stranger who none the less is myself, and whose unique function is to bear witness to what I am.

9 Beyond knowledge

In one's knowledge of oneself, one is seeking one's essence, and if it is true that one can only find it by producing it, true knowledge of someone else must necessarily be the knowledge of a man in the making, not of one that is already made. If it were not so, he would be for me a mere thing. To know another is not to cast an ineffectual eye on a finished product; true knowledge of another is a life-giving stream, bathing one who is still making himself. By the interest we show, by the questions with which we confront him, by the lessons we learn from him, we change him and are ourselves changed.

In a word, it is impossible to know another so long as one restricts oneself to the role of spectator or observer; I can only apprehend that in him by which he is becoming what he is on condition that I associate myself with it. For he becomes himself with me and through me, as I become myself with him and through him. Men attain existence together, through each other. Hence it is true that each man comes to know himself through his contact with others, and only so. And his essence is the point where every contact, real or possible, with everyone else, fuses together. So in his every action, however insignificant, the destiny of the universe and his own are indivisibly linked and involved. *yet politicians are among the most pathological of freud's concept of narcissits..*

Narcissus did not understand that all men need the mutual presence of others in order to bear the burden of existence: so long as he was left to his own devices, how could he be anything else but his own dream? Narcissus makes do with this dream: his existence drains away and finally dissolves and vanishes. This explains the melancholy which so soon invades his soul.

10 *Mutual help*

My judgements of other men are related, for the most part, to what I would like to be, and if they are cruel, it is because I am punishing myself in them. I am just or compassionate only if I judge them by what I am, and precisely at those moments when I am at my most cowardly and most contemptible. Then I sympathize with every anxious reaction of their self-love, and I am less eager to blame them than to help them. And this in turn leads me back to myself, to reconciliation with myself, with an effect which is at once tranquilizing and purifying. This is the meaning of the Gospel injunction to abstain from judging, a rule which is little practiced today. Never have men been so arrogantly ready to pass judgement, and to disparage and despise each other.

People say that we should judge other man with the same impartiality and disinterestedness as we judge things, but this is neither possible nor desirable. For we are caught up with them in mutual relationships, which, being personal, are what gives a meaning to our judgements and alone justifies them. And thus it is that character-traits which appear ugly and petty in those from whom we remain separated and who go their way without us, strike us as human, touching even, in those on whom we bestow our attention and our love, in whom we recognize what we are, and whose fate is bound up with ours. These are the relationships of election which charity offers to all men.

Every soul bears within it an aspiration which remains forever unsatisfied because the infinite is its aim. Consequently the man does not exist who is not conscious of his insufficiency; but sooner or later every other man shows him his, and the realization of this common weakness may become not only a double consolation, but a mutual stimulus. For I transcend myself the moment I go out from myself. The mere admission that I am not sufficient unto myself, that you are not sufficient unto yourself, creates between us a communion which provides each of us with what he lacked when he was alone. To know that one's wretchedness is shared is to begin to overcome it. But this is not all: a moment ago I knew of no balm for my distress, but when I applied myself to bring you comfort in yours, I found my own comfort in the act. It is precisely thus that the knowledge of another deepens self-knowledge, and the lover of another ennobles the love one bears oneself.

11 *Communication on the heights*

It is entirely false to suppose that when two persons enter into communication what they mutually transmit is what they already have. What they transmit is nothing but the power to acquire, each through the other, what neither yet possesses. What I have, I have already used, and rejected. It is of no further service to me—or to you. My aim is neither to awaken in you a state of mind which you already know all too well and which would take all heart out of you, because it would bring you back too sharply to yourself; nor, on the other hand, do I wish to awaken in you some state of mind as yet unknown to you, and which could bring you nothing more than some fleeting emotion. Genuine communication takes place only when each of the two persons is a mediator to the other, when each reveals to the other the deep, unknown desire he bears in the secret places of his heart; the discovery of another's solitude allows him both to break out of his, and to plumb its depths.

We should raise ourselves, and raise him in whose presence we are, to the highest height we can each attain by mutual help. And each of us is there like the rung of a ladder to support the other in his ascent. Only then does the presence of another man become real to us, a deeply felt and moving experience. In all other circumstances his presence is apparent only, and at best barely hides two self-interests in competition, or else indifference, tedium, and aversion.

In each of us there are several persons: there is a person created by our vanity; he is no more nor less than the spectacle he seeks to offer to the world; this person looks out upon other men with contempt or with jealousy. Then there is a timid, anxious person, who shies away from others' eyes, but only because he is conscious within himself of yet a third person, who is deeper and truer, a person who seems ever to elude him, and whom the mask which he offers to the world constantly betrays. There is no true spiritual encounter except when two persons succeed in awakening, each in the heart of the other, this hidden person, in whom they recognize themselves, but also transcend themselves, and unite together.   *Pigeon-holing*

No man asks of another to spread out before him those all-too-familiar emotions which confirm him in his present state. Perhaps no one ever forgives another for doing this. Communication with another person can only take place in a domain which is above them both, and as the result of an impulse through which each of the two, forgetful of self, and thinking only of the other with intent to help him to reach a higher plane, receives from him forthwith the very life which he is seeking to bestow. It will be said that, like mountain peaks, the higher the summit of consciousness, the more complete the loneliness. But it is to such a one the eyes of all men turn, and he alone can draw men together in unity.

Notes

1. Fr. *intimité*
2. Fr. *intimité*
3. Matt. 7:2.

CHAPTER III

THE PARADOX of sincerity lies in the fact that until I act, I do not properly exist; hence sincerity cannot be the conformity of my acts and words to any pre-existent object or being. Sincerity, like being, lies in the act itself. And yet sincerity is truth to one's essential being; the real problem is to discover the latter. (This problem will be taken up again in Chapter VII.)

On Being Oneself

❧

1 *Polyphony of consciousness*

The drama of consciousness consists in this: in order to constitute itself, it must break the unity of the self. After that, it starts an interminable struggle to reconquer this lost unity, but were it ever to succeed it would destroy itself.

It follows that consciousness, which is a dialogue with others and with the world, begins with a dialogue with oneself. We need two eyes to see and two ears to hear, as though we could not perceive anything except through the interplay of two images at once similar and different. Furthermore, neither sight nor hearing ever operates alone but only with reference to each other, or else to one of the other senses, which they stimulate, and which then contributes new information. Thus a sort of polyphony comes into being, wherein all the voices of the soul match all the voices of nature.

But we can go further: sense perception never stands alone; it always brings to birth an idea, a memory, an emotion, an intention, which in turn react upon it, and set up within us new dialogues—between present and past, past and future, universe and spirit, what we think and what we feel, what we feel and what we will. Moreover, in our consciousness there is always a gap between what we are and what we have, what we have and what we desire, a gap which we are ever seeking to close without ever quite succeeding. When I question myself with total sincerity, I find that the goal of my desire is too mobile to satisfy me, and too complex for me to be able to express it without debasing and mutilating it.

The difficulty one has in being sincere is the difficulty of being present in what one says and does, with the whole of oneself; for we divide ourselves, and show certain aspects of ourselves, none of which is the true self. But a wholly honest conscience, when deciding on a course of action, does not forget or cast away the rejected alternatives. Without wasting its strength on futile regrets on their account, it will try to introduce their positive essence and their original flavor into the chosen one.

Logic and morality have accustomed us to think and to act according to alternatives, as though one always had to say yes or no, as though there were no third possibility. But this method of proceeding suits only somewhat rigid souls, those who do not know that the third alternative does not lie between the yes and the no, but in a higher yes, one which always combines the yes and the no.

2 Cynicism

Each of us is an object of scandal for himself when, cynically comparing what he is and what he shows, he reflects that there is no man living to whom he would dare to show all the ideas which pass through his consciousness, even though they flicker and are gone. He feels indeed that he himself could not consider them too nearly without shame.

The reason is that all humanity dwells in each man, the best and the worst. True sincerity does not consist in considering as real and our own all the obscure impulses, the unformed desires, the vague temptations which flit across our minds. They are not ours until we have begun to dwell upon them and to give them some consistency. True sincerity is to pass through them, to descend into the depths of ourselves, there to discover what we want to be. There is an apparent sincerity which consists in laying bare to our horrified gaze all that we think we are, which in fact is nothing but what we might become if we were suddenly to relax our vigilance. Consciousness contains within itself the ambiguity of every possibility. It becomes the source of discouragement and frustration if one conceives of it as a fully-fledged reality rather than the power which constructs this reality. And so, to be sincere is not to be content to become conscious of one's inchoate desires, and to body them forth in words before ever performing the inner act which alone makes them ours. It is only when we consent to them that we can be judged.

And so it is that sincerity often appears like a conversion, when we recognize that our life is bad, but are already beginning to show that it is good. This is why it is said that he who makes a confession which changes him triumphs over the shame of the confession. If the light in which we bathe and purify our past reconciles us to our past, it is because it compels our past actions to conjure up in our minds a potentiality of which we intend to make better use in the future. And we should not be surprised that the man for whom we feel the keenest and the most passionate interest should not be he who is exempt from all the vices, but he who, though continuing to feel their stab, sharpens against them the cutting edge of his whole spiritual life.

3 *Play-acting for one's own benefit*

It is the man who thinks who is in most danger of play-acting before an audience consisting of himself. He is never satisfied with what he finds in himself. He spoils it by constantly thinking about it. His true being is always, for him, somewhere other than in his present being; he never manages to distinguish what he imagines from what he feels. He can make out scores of different characters in himself. He imagines scores of possibilities, stretching out in every direction beyond the reality which has been given him. He must needs resolutely turn his face towards the latter and concentrate his attention upon it, though often all that is required is a touch of simplicity and a little love; with these he would make contact with it, almost without trying.

All this is not difficult to explain. When I look at myself, another is there, and he is the spectator to whom I am exhibiting myself; further, this spectator always resembles a stranger, for whom I can never be anything but a mere appearance: I have ceased to be a person; I am a thing, an "image" which I deliberately compose.

The dialogue in which Narcissus engages inevitably contains an element of duplicity: to be double is the very nature of consciousness. And the difference between what I am and what I show is the product of reflection and of my effort to be sincere. And so I have the impression that I never am. Sincerity is always a problem; no one can rightly estimate another's, or his own.

4 Deception is impossible

In a man's relationships with other men, an apparently real being springs up, and always takes the place of the real one. This is an abdication and a humiliation of the self which often passes unnoticed; we use a dishonorable subterfuge to disguise what has happened. For our real being seeks ever to take advantage of the high opinion in which our apparent being is held.

But can I really hope that men will take the appearance that I show for the reality that I am? In every one of my words and acts the hallmark of self-love is to be observed, unmistakable to all, though people sometimes allow one to think the contrary; or else I betray a sense of guilt, which, indeed, everyone is expecting, waiting for, and yet it serves no useful purpose; but the others pounce on it, some to bring me help, and others to crush me.

Dissimulation is more difficult than people think. One's body, one's voice, one's eyes, one's face do not merely bear witness to what one is; they are one's very being, and to a fairly perspicacious observer they reveal our most secret intention, even the intention to reveal nothing, which recalls the legend of the Nordic maiden, the jewel in whose ring would change color every time she told a lie.[1] So it is with the boldest, the most brazen countenance. And if the face were to remain immobile, the eyes, which are subtler, would change; or failing the eyes, there would be a disturbance in that almost imperceptible harmony of all the features, which is the stamp of a man's perfect naturalness.

People are forever talking of refusing to exhibit their inner feelings, of reserve, of reticence. But in reality they are equally incapable of doing this and of not doing it. For sincerity is ambiguous, and it is true that the two most difficult things in the world are showing oneself and hiding oneself. Often there is nothing harder than to show another the very thing I want him to see. The degree of sincerity I can achieve depends on him as much as on me. Over and beyond the sincerity which the individual may consciously strive for, there is another sincerity, which only friends can recognize and experience.

Inversely, dissimulation also presupposes the complicity of two people, each of whom is prepared to accept as more real what the other shows than what he is hiding, and each of whom refuses to admit to himself that his real concern is with what he is trying to hide, but which always comes to the surface in one way or another, together with the desire to hide it.

But again, it sometimes happens that a man deceives himself before he sets about deceiving others. Self-love gets the better of him before he begins getting the better of other people. He experiments first on himself, measuring the success he can hope for with others by the success he has with himself. Even when he fails, he keeps up the same desperate enterprise. For men have agreed to live in a world of appearance and pretense. It is in this world that their words echo back and forth, although truth in its entirety is there before their eyes, nor do they fail to recognize it. They are fully conscious of this inconsistency; it may even give them a cruel delight.

5 *Gyges' ring*

How is it possible, it may be asked, not to be sincere, if my being coincides with my acts even more closely than with my thoughts? If my acts perfectly express what all men see, what difference could there be between what I appear and what I am?

Let us leave aside the insincerity which is a deliberate intention to put people on the wrong scent: it deceives none but the obtuse; and it never deceives the deceiver. It is nothing but a trick which I adopt on the spur of the moment to achieve a certain effect; but the intention to produce this effect leaves an impression on him who uses it, and this will not be effaced.

Men know perfectly well that they cannot hide any part of what they are, and if they possessed Gyges' ring, that is precisely what they would wish it to accomplish for them. This ring would make our body invisible, thus enabling us to achieve in the world of visible things an effect whose cause was invisible, and not of this world: this would certainly be the first miracle. But the miracle would only be complete if the ring, while making us invisible to others, made us also perfectly interior and perfectly transparent to ourselves; if, in short, it made the myth of Narcissus at the fountain come true.

Fortunately the ring has not been vouchsafed us. It would be the supreme temptation. The anguish of existence and the secret of responsibility reside at that precise point at which, before the eyes of the world, we convert into an act which leaves an indelible trace upon the world, a possibility which previously had no existence except for us. But since they do not possess the ring, most men struggle desperately to produce an image of themselves, by means of their words, their silence and their works—an image which represents not what they are, nor even what they would like to be, but what they wish people to believe they are.

6 *Sim ut sum aut non sim*[2]

The highest duty, the most subtle difficulty, the gravest responsibility is to be all that one is, to assume full responsibility for it, and for all the consequences. Frankness sets me free and gives me the courage I need. It is falsehood which binds me. The function of consciousness is to force me to take possession of myself. And this taking possession resembles a creation, since it consists of giving reality to a potential being which has, so to say, been put at our disposal. But to remain as a potentiality is not to be. I can then, if I choose, not be; I can refuse to accept the existence which is ceaselessly offered me. But what I cannot do is to become other than what I am. It is inconceivable that I should become other than I am without my self being annihilated. Falsehood is the self's refusal of its being.

To be what one is—nothing is more difficult than this for the man who has begun to think, to reflect, and to distinguish, however imperfectly, between his nature and his liberty. Will he follow nothing but his nature, while disapproving of it, suffering under it oftentimes, and occasionally condemning it outright? Or on the other hand will he put his trust in his judgement and in the freedom of his will, as though he had no nature? But one's nature will not be forgotten: merely to ignore it is not to reduce it to silence. Nature it is who puts at our disposal every potentiality we have; sincerity first recognizes them, then sets them to work.

To be sincere is to descend into the depths of our selves, and there to find the gifts which are ours, and yet which are nothing except by virtue of the use we make of them. It is refusing to let them lie unused. It is preventing them remaining buried within us, in the darkness of the realm of possibility. It is bringing them forth into the light of day, so that, in the view of all, they increase the wealth of the world, by being, as it were, a revelation which continually enriches it. Sincerity is the act by which, at one and the same time, a man knows himself and makes himself. It is the act by which he shows himself to be what he is, and consents to contribute, according to the measure of his strength, to the work of creation.

7 *Discovering what I am*

In our relationships with others, sincerity is an attempt to abolish all distinction between our real and our manifest selves; but the ultimate sincerity is sincerity in our relationship with ourselves. It consists not so much in showing oneself as one is as in discovering what one is. It demands of us that we should penetrate below and beyond all the superficial layers of consciousness, the domain of fleeting impressions, into that mysterious region where are born those deep desires which we acknowledge as our own, and which are our life's contact with the absolute. Introspection produces the best effects or the worst, according to where we look, and the intention which motivates our looking. Either we dwell upon our passing impressions (in which we are always unduly interested); or else we penetrate to their place of origin, and, in so doing, we free ourselves from our slavery to them.

Real sincerity is to compel myself to be myself; to become what I am. It is to search for my essence, which begins to lose its purity the moment I look outside myself for the motives of my actions. For this essence is not an object which I can observe, but a creation which I am bringing into being; it is the act whereby I give effect to certain potentialities which are in me, and which wither away if I cease to exercise them.

Sincerity is an act involving, indivisibly, entering into oneself and going out from oneself, a quest which is from the first a discovery; a commitment which is from the first a self-transcendence; a waiting for a voice which from the first was calling; an opening of the heart which from the first was an act of faith in a revelation as yet undisclosed, but ever on the point of breaking forth. Sincerity is the link between what I am and what I intend to be.

It may be said that it is a virtue of the heart and not of the intelligence. "For where your heart is, there is your true treasure."[3] Which suffices to explain why sincerity brings with it infinitely more reward than the most glittering sham.

8 *A sword through the heart*

A sword must go through one's heart,[4] says Saint Luke, if one is to pierce through to one's deepest thoughts; but only innocence can wield this sword. It is quite wrong to say that innocence sees no evil; it discerns, and then tears away, all the veils with which self-love covers our naked being. But this is the way of virtue which, as Plato says, knows virtue and vice, whereas vice knows vice only.

Sincerity consists in that tranquil courage which enables us to enter into existence as we truly are. But a double fear nearly always holds one back, fear of the very power one has at one's disposal, and fear of being exposed to public opinion. It is the passage from the hidden into the manifest world which creates our perplexity.

But we are too concerned with appearances. If I am what I ought to be within, I will also be so without. It is true that a capacity for stripping one's soul bare is called for, a capacity which I do not possess at all times. Sometimes I am not granted enough light. Sometimes I am not sufficiently present to myself. I am not always ready to speak or to act. Often I must be content to wait. Sincerity calls for much discretion and much silence.

The mere thought of another man watching has a paralyzing effect upon us. It can make us ashamed of that very quality wherein lies our superiority, if he questions it, or fails to recognize its worth. But when we are alone, we should act as though the eyes of the world were upon us; and when they are, we should act as though we were alone. Indeed, vanity itself, if only it were great enough, could not be satisfied with appearance, which, however, almost always is all that it feeds on: it should dissolve itself in the ocean of its own exacting demands, seeking no satisfaction other than that which perfect sincerity would afford it. It is a weak and miserable kind of vanity which imagines that appearance can go one better than being; and yet, it is within the power of vanity to transcend itself continually, and even to become its exact opposite, when a man refuses to allow his being ever to fall short of his manifested appearance.

There are two sorts of men: those whose ears are tuned to self-love, and whose eyes are fixed upon the image of themselves they offer to the world; and those who cannot imagine that such an image exists, or, if it exists, that it can differ from what they are.

9 *Beyond myself*

Sincerity lays an obligation upon me to withhold everything in me which belongs to me and me alone, and to manifest everything in me which resembles a revelation whose interpreter I am. It follows that, if I am sincere, I can express only what is indeed within me, but always as though it were not of me. Sincerity expresses at one and the same time what is most interior to ourselves, and what is farthest removed from ourselves, namely the truth with which we are entrusted.

You say, "I am sincere," and you think that you have thereby justified what you say and what you do. But what does your sincerity mean to me if it is the sincerity of nothing, if it communicates nothing but the reactions of your self-love, and the pathetic expressions of your weakness and your wretchedness? And yet you present this sincerity of yours as an excuse and as a matter of pride. "This is what I am. I am frank about myself. And this being that I offer to your gaze has, like you, its place in the world, and the same sun shines upon it with the same light."

But this flaunted sincerity of yours is often nothing but a sham, of no interest either to yourself or to anybody else: it awakens no echo in me if it communicates nothing more than a fact which neither you nor I can grasp and hold firm. The sincerity which I am looking for, and the only one I need, the only one which brings my eyes to bear on a destiny, in yourself and in myself, which is private to each of us and which is yet common to us both, is not the attempt, however genuine, to describe yourself as a thing; it is rather a resolve to seek yourself, to affirm yourself, and to begin even now to commit yourself, the determination to penetrate to the very essence of the real wherein each of us is rooted, and to recognize by unmistakable signs what is required of you, namely the task which you have to accomplish, and to which you are even now beginning to put your hand.

10 *Sincerity and truth*

It is common belief that there is nothing in the world easier than being sincere, and that all that is required is not to alter to the smallest degree reality such as it has been given to us. To lie or to dissimulate, in this view, is to intervene, to bring one's will into play, to substitute for my real self a false self which is entirely different. Is it not true, it will be said, that to be sincere is to be content to let things be what they are?

But the problem is not so easy. The moment I begin to speak or to act, the moment my eyes open to the light, I add something to the real, and modify it. This modification is nothing less than the creation of a spectacle without which the real would not exist for me. It is when I look out upon the world that it comes to birth before my eyes, like a view which takes its contours from the perspective in which it is seen, and from the constant play of lights and shadows upon it. And yet no one would contend that the real world is created by myself, by my act which apprehends it. It has certain characteristics which I must accept whether I like it or not, and which I can check against the experience of other men. Thus it is that I can distinguish error from truth.

But sincerity is not truth. For example, the painter translates by his art, with varying degrees of sincerity, his entirely personal vision of the universe; and it is only this vision that one can qualify as true. And yet no one would agree that to be sincere is to reproduce my own vision of things, just as it is; while on the other hand that to be true is to reproduce, within this vision itself, things just as they are. For it is in the *quality* of the vision that my sincerity consists. It lies in my effort to make it ever more delicate, more penetrating, and more profound.

Truth is a light which bathes everything that is, and which enlightens me provided I open my eyes. One may say that sincerity is nothing more than simply consenting to this light, provided one adds that the truth which is in question here is the very truth of what I am, and further that it is not enough that I should contemplate this truth, but I must first of all bring it into being.

The commonly accepted view is that truth is the coincidence of thought and reality. But how could such a coincidence be possible so long as the real is something other than myself? If, on the other hand, sincerity is the coincidence of ourselves with ourselves, how is it possible to miss it? Nevertheless *amour-propre* achieves just this. The essence of sincerity is to conquer *amour-propre*. And one may say that, unlike truth, the search for which is the attempt to make the act of my consciousness conform to the spectacle presented by things, sincerity is the attempt to make the spectacle which I offer to the world conform to the act of my consciousness.

It would thus seem that sincerity alone is capable of resolving the duality of object and subject which philosophers have made the supreme condition of all knowledge. If Narcissus went down to destruction, it was because he actually tried to *create* this duality in his very being. For he thought he could see himself and enjoy himself before he had acted and before he had made himself. He lacked the courage to engage upon the splendid and unique venture wherein action precedes being and determines it—that creative activity of which mathematics offers us a model in the realm of pure knowledge, and inner sincerity a dramatic application to ourselves.

11 Sincerity in action

To be sincere is to show oneself, but at the same time as one is making oneself. It is not to talk but to act. Unfortunately one is always inclined to water down the meaning of the word "sincerity," reducing it to the idea of speaking about oneself truthfully. But how can one speak truthfully about a being who is still in the making, whose every word and every action adds something to what he is? And who can claim to be able to tell the truth about himself without a tremor, or without the blush which both perverts the truth and debases the self?

But sincerity must reach out, beyond all speech, to an invisible inner life,[5] which speech may always betray, for it can only trace its shadow. Sincerity appears only when this inner life[6] begins to be incarnated in acts which determine both our being and our destiny.

Sincerity does not consist in reproducing a good likeness of a pre-existent reality. It is itself creative. It is a virtue shown forth in action, not merely in the act of expression. Our self is nothing more than a bundle of virtualities: it is for us to realize them. True sincerity is an accomplishment. And it is quite conceivable that one should miss it, whether through laziness or through fear, or because one finds it easier or more expedient to yield to public opinion and to renounce oneself, letting oneself be dragged unresistingly down the slope of social conformity.

In sincerity, the act by which we find ourselves and the act by which we make ourselves are one and the same. Sincerity is at once the attention which arouses our potentialities, and the courage which gives them form, without which they would be nothing. Potentiality is the voice within us; our courage is our response. Sincerity consists not merely, as is imagined, of examining with pitiless lucidity one's own secret thoughts; it compels this same inner being to cross its own frontiers, to take its place in the world, and there to manifest what it is.

12   *The return to the source*

From the moment I begin to act, my life is imprisoned in a situation. It bears the weight of its past; countless forces begin to sweep it along; it is caught up in a movement; and I cannot tell whether I am carried by this movement or whether I am producing it. But sincerity challenges all the voices which call to me from without, and commands me to descend into my heart's heart. It is always a return to the source. It makes me a being perpetually being born.

Sincerity liberates us from every preoccupation with public opinion or with the effect we are producing. It brings us back to our own origin, showing us to ourselves as we were when we left the Creator's hands, when life first flashed forth, and before outer appearances had begun to seduce us, or we had learned the art of pretending.

It shows us to ourselves as we are, and not in a portrait which would necessarily be something outside ourselves. It needs no oaths or promises to carry conviction. It is a perfect transparency in the eyes which casts no shadow between you and me; nor does the remembrance of things past or the desire of things to come cast any shadow between us; again it is rectitude of a will which admits no duplicity, no evasion, and no dissembling, between a man and other men.

Sincerity is a spiritual nobility. For the sincere man seeks to live under the open sky. He alone has enough self-respect to hide nothing from himself, and to expect nothing except from the truth; he alone is not content merely to appear, but establishes himself so firmly in being that for him being is indistinguishable from appearance.

13   *Under the eye of God*

Sincerity is the act by which I put myself under the eye of God; there is no other sincerity. For of God alone may it be said that outward appearance is as though it were not. He is himself the pure presence of everything that is. When I turn to Him, everything in me but what I am ceases to count.

For God is not only the ever-open eye, from whom I can hide nothing of what I know about myself; but He is also the light which pierces the darkness, revealing me to myself as I have always been without knowing it. Self-love which hid me from myself is a garment which suddenly drops off. Another love folds me about, one which makes my soul itself transparent.

As long as life remains in us, we nurse the hope that we can change what we are, or conceal it. But once it is threatened or near its end, nothing counts but what we are. One is only perfectly sincere in the presence of death, because death is irrevocable, and, by terminating our existence, confers upon it the character of the absolute. That is what is expressed in the picture of the judge whose eye misses nothing, and who, at the moment of our death, sees into the remotest corners of our soul. What is the truth behind this idea of the Divine Eye? Is it not that it is now impossible for us to add anything to what we have made, to escape from ourselves into any future, and to continue to make a distinction between our real and manifested being? And since this is the moment when the will loses its power, it is now impossible to avoid confronting the spectacle of our being in its finished state, our being which, up to this moment, had been nothing more than a rough sketch, susceptible of endless additions and corrections?

To be sincere, we must not merely think of God as a witness: we must take Him as a model. For sincerity does not consist merely in seeing our selves in His light, but in making ourselves in conformity with His will. What am I but what He wishes me to be? And yet, there immediately appears before me an infinite disparity between what I do and this power within me which, in spite of everything, it is my one aspiration to exercise. And indeed I constantly fail, and in exact proportion to my failure I become, for myself and for others, a mere appearance, dissipated by a puff of wind, and finally annihilated by death.

This is the sense in which we should take the words: "Whoever disowns me in this world, I will disown him before my Father; whoever acknowledges me in this world, I will acknowledge him before my Father. I came into the world to bear witness to the truth."[7]

Notes

1. The story runs that, mistrusting her capacity to tell the truth, she refrained from speech altogether, thus betraying what she wished to hide.

2. "Let me be what I am, or let me not be."

3. Lavelle's adaptation of Luke 12:34.

4. *ibid.*, 2:35.

5. Fr. *intimité*.

6. *idem.*

7. Here Lavelle adapts and combines two texts: Christ to the disciples (Matt. 10:32–3) and to Pilate (John 18:37).

CHAPTER IV

REALITY is spirit, and invisible; effective actions in the material world are necessary if the self is to create itself, though the material effects (which is all we see) are, as it were, secondary and derivative, and this for two different reasons: the first, that the effects take place in the space-time world, which passes away; the second, that there is an order of the world, the expression of the Pure Act, which, though leaving us free to make our mark upon the world, yet overrules, counterbalances, and integrates individual actions, and so maintains itself, a sort of divine ecology.

It follows that there is a sense in which it would be true to say that being is more important than doing, the will poised to act more important than the act itself, the discovery of one's essence more important than the act which creates it.

In the final stage of the soul's development, act and being come together and are one. At this point, the soul's essence is fixed; will and choice are no longer necessary; act, being, knowledge, communion, and love are fused into a virtually indistinguishable whole. Even in the material world—in life in time—matter is now barely necessary to mediate them.

Life is a journey towards this goal.

Visible and Invisible Action

❧

1 *Fields of responsibility*

All action expresses us and misrepresents us at one and the same time. It is the expression and the manifestation of our deepest being. But it is also its testing and its proving. And we never become entirely ourselves until we go out from ourselves to act, until we leave the domain of pure virtuality to take our place in the world and assume responsibility.

We are responsible, in the first place, for our thoughts. For just as the intention is prior to the act, so the thought is prior to the intention which rises from it: responsibility can always be carried back a step further. It takes its rise at the point where consciousness begins to take shape. But it becomes more precise at each stage of the uninterrupted development in the course of which it brings into play the means by which it is fulfilled, and takes to itself a body which makes it manifest to every eye. Now, since the essence of responsibility is to separate me from the world and to make me accountable for it, I am in some way responsible both for what you think and what you do, so that responsibility grows ever more subtle; no limit can be set to it.

There is no such thing as an insignificant act, that is to say an act which does not involve our responsibility and affect the whole order of the spiritual universe. It is not to be wondered at therefore that responsibility always meets with opposing forces, without which it could not come to birth, enabling our action to be our own, in other words to break with what is spontaneous and instinctive in ourselves. But those opposing forces are in us, and not merely in the universe without us. Over and above the difficulty which every man encounters in his attempt to render things obedient to his touch, he faces a more formidable difficulty—that of creating himself, and this means finding himself.

2 Assuming responsibility

The weakest sort of men try to evade responsibility before acting, and disclaim it when they have acted. They put more effort into exonerating themselves than into avoiding the necessity of doing so. However, since they expect to be called to account when they have done something wrong, they refuse to accept responsibility for what they have done except when the event appears to justify them. They do not recognize their responsibility for the destiny of the universe before they act, and they allow others to hold them responsible for it only when the universe has already pronounced in their favor.

At the opposite end of the scale are those particularly virile natures who seize this burden, both before and after the event. They claim it insistently; they would increase it. At the moment of action they feel that everything depends on them alone. After action, they reproach themselves for not having done enough. With a sort of fiery pride, they attribute to themselves a kind of omnipotence which they persist in thinking they have not used to full advantage. They care too little for others, or else they have too poor an opinion of them, to concede them the smallest share of influence in the issue of the enterprise. Success, they assume, will come as a matter of course—they hardly give it a thought. But failure, even others' failure if they are guided by charity, distresses them, makes them anxious in the extreme, and inconsolable. However remote they may be from the scene of action, they feel accountable for the whole world, and they insist on bearing the guilt of all the evil in it. They will not share responsibility, either with God or with their neighbor. For they look so deeply within themselves and with such penetrating sincerity, that they always find resources in themselves which they have not used. The thought that grace may have failed them never crosses their minds: they know that it is whole and indivisible, and they are forever afraid that they have not been worthy of it, or have failed to be equal to its demands.

But the most truly courageous man of all, he who always takes upon himself the responsibility for a failure, who always imagines that he has failed to use the necessary means, that he has lacked decisiveness or constancy, recognizes, too, that apparent failure may indeed be apparent only, that he would be wrong to judge it by the grief he feels, or by the difference between the intention and the event, the true criterion being the spiritual fruit which the act has produced. He is assured that nothing can happen in the world which is not the effect of a secret justice whose scales are infinitely more accurate than those of our sensibility, a justice which obeys laws of unlimited flexibility, but as rigorous as those which determine the fall of an apple.

3 In praise of work

The ancient Greeks said that the gods took vengeance on Prometheus for having taught men to work, in other words, to transform matter with their hands, at the same time leaving the mark of their spirit upon it: they were afraid that men would turn away and cease to worship them. Thus work was thought of as a rebellion against God before it was thought of as a punishment coming from God.[1]

But there is another way of looking at work. Proudhon called it the visible manifestation of mental activity: it is the expression of the creative act, and continues the creative work of God. One might call it the streaming forth of spirit, spirit prevailing over matter and not being prevailed against. In work the spirit is liberated. And it forms the person in the process of transforming things; it humanizes and spiritualizes the person in the process of modifying material objects. And finally, it draws men together in the pursuit of a goal which is visible to all, and in the construction of the world in which they are called to live.

That is why work, in which a man turns from thought (which exists nowhere but in the mind) to action (which affects the organization of the created world), always tends to become work in common. And in all work, man's object is the goal aimed at and not himself, and beyond the goal, his neighbor, whom he addresses by this means. Your conscientiousness is your effort tested and measured by its effects. And the finest death a man can die is to die out of devotion to the work he has undertaken.

4 Activity and achievement

So long as we are active, we are delivered from all the servitudes of the body and the soul. We do not know what the outcome will be, although we know that work is never without results; nor are we thinking of the rules which we are supposed to observe, although we know that we cannot transgress them. There are not two forms of activity, material and spiritual, for there is no movement of the body which cannot be spiritualized, just as any spiritual inspiration may fade away, to become, finally, a mere physical habit.

It is pointless to imagine the existence of pure activity, independent of the body, and not submitted to the resistance and the acid test of things; but the question remains: which is the means and which the end? It is superstitious to imagine that the goal of activity is nothing but the transformation of the physical world, after which one should, as it were, seek to disappear in the perfection of one's handiwork. The spirit having accomplished its task, passes on; the thing it created was nothing more than the material in which it operated and the instrument of its progress.

Space is the road to all its triumphs, but it is not here that it makes its abiding city. It is because our activity leaves its traces as it passes through the world of space that the world can be subjected to it. But this victory of the spirit is in constant danger of being turned into defeat, for it leads us to think that its function is to dominate matter, as in industry. We become caught up in a round of measuring, producing and increasing all those visible effects which, without us, would not be. However, in mastering things we are mastered by them. We exult in the ease and the self-confidence which come to us when we act upon them in obedience to the implacable laws which unfailingly produce ever the same effects. But an activity where men have at their disposal a sophisticated technique for acting upon things, finding their ultimate satisfaction in it and concentrating all their thoughts on its perfecting, has become the servant of this technique. It is an activity from which life has departed.

5 *The birds of the air and the lilies of the field*

We read in Matthew[2] "Take no thought, saying, What shall we eat?" and yet this is the main preoccupation of almost every man, of the adolescent from the moment he leaves the parental roof, and of the old man who has but a step to take to reach the grave. What shall we eat? ask the professors of political economy. They would laugh to scorn anyone who sought to imitate the birds of the air or the lilies of the field. Which of us indeed would dare to imitate them without a touch of anxiety?

But we misunderstand what is asked of us. For to live like the birds and the lilies is to listen faithfully to every call within, and to respond obediently to every call coming from without; it is to begin our lives all over again at every instant; it is to entrust the results of our actions to an order which transcends us, and which we can neither alter nor control. Not that we should leave everything to Fate out of sloth or despair, the slaves of our temperament, be it optimistic or pessimistic. On the contrary, we must exercise our will in all its strength, adapting it precisely and accurately to the specific circumstances. As for the results, they do not depend on us but on the order which rules the world, an order which can never be violated, though it is for us to collaborate in maintaining it. Moreover this order still triumphs even when, from the disorder of our wills, arises the disorder of things.

Humanity's greatest error, particularly in our own age, is to imagine that by means of an external effect one can obtain the supreme good; this resides alone in an operation which the soul must accomplish. Men make enjoyment their supreme goal. But they expend immense exterior activity creating the instruments by which to come by anything and everything, while turning away from that inner activity which would free them from the bondage to these instruments, and without which they cannot even take possession of the things they create.

Men's unhappiness often comes not from acting too little but from acting too much, or at the wrong moment. They thereby produce in the natural order the effects which they have willed but which, though satisfying some present desire, do violence to other, deeper desires; these erupt when it is too late, causing some terrible upheaval which they had not foreseen, and under which they may be buried.

6 Invisible action

The only action which is real, effective and beneficial, is that which works invisibly. Many men think the contrary; for them, the essence of all action is to change things, to make them conform to their desires. But it often falls out that this sort of action, though it transforms the face of the world, takes the place of real action, which changes spirits, and is made to stand in its stead.

The deepest sort of action is also the most secret. It seems to produce no effect; and yet it penetrates farthest of all, with a radiation which the senses cannot register. It seems to be independent of the body, although in fact it transfigures it. Its perfection consists in giving rise to nothing but other actions, which appear to come to birth spontaneously and to be their own object; no one sees the source from which these actions spring.

It is right and good that true activity should always be invisible. It is right and good that the secret we bear within us can never be violated, that the original source of everything we do should be hidden from all eyes, that these calm waters should remain untroubled and unstained, and that when we begin to intervene in the work of the creation it should be with such gentle tranquillity that it is impossible for anyone to imagine that it has just suffered a change, or to recognize in what has happened the work of our hands.

The eyes of the body are capable of seeing events only, in other words movements; they cannot pierce through to their significance, namely the motive and the intention which produce them. The outward appearance of an action cannot but be the same, whether it be done out of egoism or out of love. No visible sign distinguishes the purest sacrifice from an act of base selfishness. For it is only the eye of the spirit which can make matter transparent and penetrate through it to the spiritual truth of which it is an expression, but which it also hides from view. Among those who perform the same deeds and who appear to be inspired by the same thoughts, some are the slaves of self-interest and self-love, while for others life is a perpetual self-giving. The faces, speech, attitudes, habitual gestures may look alike to him who takes note of nothing but bodies. In the same way, during the winter season, the dead trees cannot be distinguished from the living. And yet there are certain subtle signs which bear witness to the presence of life in the latter, and which are recognizable only to him who bears life in himself, and who, when he looks out from himself, is attentive to nothing else. But even so it may happen that those trees which have most sap, and which, at the appointed season, will be loaded with leaves, flowers and fruit, still deceive the most experienced and careful observer.

Perfection is attained only when the difference between material and spiritual activity is abolished; or again when, in contra-distinction to the natural order, material activity becomes invisible and spiritual activity visible.

7 *Act of presence*

The most effective action of all is an act of pure presence, and every effort we make to reinforce it, or to add something to it, is a mark of its imperfection and insufficiency. In action, our sole purpose is to become present to reality, to ourselves, to others, or to God. Now, all presence is spiritual, although one can only reach it by passing through the material, and going beyond. But it may happen that the world of sense apparently brings us complete satisfaction, and we ask for nothing more. We think it absolves us—though at times it actually prevents us—from performing the personal and living act which alone could bring us spiritual presence. On the other hand, when spiritual presence is born, we have no further need of the other. We must not be guilty of the weakness of desiring it.

The statement that a man can act merely by his presence means that the effects of his actions come about without his having to wish it. It is thus that God rules the world. And it is thus that each of us proceeds when his actions are the simplest and the best. Then the whole of our activity develops and comes to fruition with such ease and naturalness that we might say that we are borne along by it, together, even, with the impulse in which it originated. And so we should not be surprised that so soon as the will intervenes, it runs the risk of obstructing it in its efforts to promote it.

The most perfect activity is always experienced as a pure consent to being and to living. His works, for such a man, are but a fuel, which he must ever consume, so that he may ceaselessly seek fresh fire from the original source.

8 *Perfect simplicity*

True simplicity is invisible. It is all purity, all transparency. It alone abolishes the difference between being and appearance. It transforms the most difficult things into the most natural. Most men have no other idea than to imprint upon the world a mark or sign of their passage. But every appearance perishes; and the man who, out of a desire to offer himself as a spectacle to others, is preoccupied with appearances, will perish with them. Simplicity knows no world but the inner world; it has no eyes for the outer. The best, according to the Tao, is not to do great things or to present a great image of oneself; rather, it is to leave no trace in the world of appearances; which can be interpreted to mean: not to cast any shadow, and to keep unimpaired the integrity of one's pure being.

Men almost always are vaguely aware that the good must resemble the rediscovery of an invisible order which normally passes unnoticed. This order is a sort of spiritual equilibrium, in which each thing occupies the place to which it belongs, an equilibrium which is not upset by any desire, any regret, any emotion caused by selfishness or hate. But men love to be seen. They think they exalt themselves by violating this order instead of by confirming it. And even if, with this end in view, they have to be evil or perverse, many, who are incapable of being so, like to pretend they are.

The most effective action, which is also the most generous, possesses a silent inevitability; it confounds and surpasses in efficacy every calculation. It is, one might say, without movement and without object, and yet it infallibly reaches its goal. It is the type of action which the world challenges and declares to be impossible, thus preventing it from being performed. But the wisest and strongest men feel no need to defend it, nor even to describe it. Their role is to practice it, and bring it into the light.

All our potentialities are born and rise into our consciousness in silence and solitude. The tree nourishes with its sap all the fruit it is capable of bearing; but it does not know them; it is not for the tree to see them or to taste them.

9 *Silence and speech*
Silence may be due to prudence: by keeping silent one hopes

to avoid being judged, or to avoid committing oneself. But it may also be due to asceticism: one restrains the spontaneity of one's natural reactions; one abandons the desire to make an impression on others, to win their regard, or exert an influence upon them.

Further, silence is a sort of homage which a man renders to the seriousness of life; for words merely create a world of their own, intermediate between those private feelings of ours which have no meaning for anyone but ourselves—a meaning which they always misrepresent—and the acts which change the face of the world, for which they are often substituted. The frivolous man is content to talk, but his words do not translate his thought, nor do they commit him to any line of conduct. The serious man is he who speaks least; for him the choice is between meditation and action.

Words have value on the sole condition that they mediate between the potentiality of thought and the reality of action. Further, it may be said that they make thought real, though they are also nothing but potential actions.

It is because words disclose our thought, and, once uttered, have given it a form, that they begin to bind us. They are not to be identified with a genuine act; nevertheless they create an expectation of one, and prefigure it; we are unfaithful if we do not accomplish it. Thus, words put chains about our liberty, and one must be sparing of one's words if one is to prevent them from interfering with it—if one desires one's liberty to remain ever an original beginning, and a relationship, forever new, between a will forever coming to be and a situation which is ever unpredictable.

A word, once spoken, suffices to change the state of things, but without appearing to do so. It upsets the relationship between two persons, even when it does not bring to light anything which they did not already know; the point is precisely that it brings it into the light. What was once merely a latent possibility, still in suspense, has now come into the open. What existed only in my soul has emerged without. No one can avoid taking it into account, and henceforward the whole of my conduct is conditioned by it.

And yet there remains eternally an infinite distance between what I am in my silence and what I can manifest or express. Silence has a mysterious power, which is the power of what I am, and which is always greater than the power of what I say. This inner silence, this absence of all concern for the spectacle I may be offering, gives each man to himself, and saves him from hesitation and from pretense.

And so it sometimes happens that my silence brings me closer to you than my speech.

The deepest love does not have recourse to speech. In its subtlest, as in its most passionate forms, to break silence would be to break the love; the attempt to give it a voice would weaken it. Where love is, it is one, total, and indivisible. I cannot express it without dividing it, without preferring to its incomparable presence a sign which always falls short of the reality.

Thus it is with every action one performs; and even with education, which, though it seems to make use of words, depends in the first place on a pure presence, ever active and ever offered, and which is such that it need use no pressure to fix the pupil's attention, nor any appeal to elicit a response.

10 *The face in sleep*

No spiritual potentiality maintains itself in existence other than by the acts which it performs; without them, it wilts and finally ceases to exist. There is thus much vanity in the notion that one should keep one's powers in their pristine state, as though their use were to wear them out, corrupt them or dissipate them. The moment one ceases to exercise them they are nothing. What is an interior disposition unattested by any act? In this sense I am what I do, and not what I am capable of; the latter is often merely what I think I could do.

Shall we say that in sleep it is my consciousness which drowses off, becoming suddenly quiescent, sluggish and inert? But is not the essence of consciousness to be awake, active and alive? And if the face did not bear witness to a hidden potentiality which one person has and another has not, where would be the difference between an intelligent man and a fool, when both were asleep? But, in fact, nothing but acts proceeding from their potentialities will make it possible to distinguish between them. He who keeps a potentiality all his life without using it is indistinguishable from the fool. The only difference is that he is responsible for his folly; one might say that he is a voluntary fool. But who would ever claim to be able unerringly to draw a line of demarcation between these two brands of folly?

And yet the essence of a person is an indestructible unity which, so far from being reflected, is misrepresented by individual character traits and by isolated words and actions. It is said that movement expresses personality; perhaps, but it divides it too. But when a person is absolutely still, one can discern an infinity of movements, real and possible, which counterbalance each other, enabling us to grasp the unity of his essence in a single glance, enclosed and, as it were, arrested in its totality within its own limits, before any manifestation has fragmented it and exteriorized it.

A mask is but a feigned immobility. A face is an immobility which is alive, prefiguring, and indeed beginning, a host of movements, which are all the more meaningful since the man is not obliged to complete them.

One can easily understand therefore that it has been said that the true face of a man is only revealed in sleep. He has ceased to act; he cannot keep watch upon himself; his will is suspended. We now see him not in what he does but in what he is, in other words in everything he wants to do. Now he appears with the calm of a god, miraculously delivered from all the preoccupations of his humanity; now pursued, and as it were crushed, by this same humanity. Now his face is furrowed by a wrinkle or a deep crease, created by hatred or disgust, marks which the exigencies of action or the presence of other men are sufficient to disguise or to efface for a moment. It is the fear of being found out that makes a man seek privacy to sleep.

11 *Our essence becomes definitive*

What shall I do with existence during the long interval of time which, I always tend to imagine, still separates me from death—this stretch of time, in which everything will depend on what may be given me, but still more on the way I receive it? There is a fundamental rule which I must keep ever before my eyes, namely, that my life's every action, my mind's every thought, my body's every movement should be, as it were, a commitment and a creation of my being, an expression of a decision taken, and of my determination to be what these proclaim. This must also be true of every sentence I speak or write, whereas so often I am content merely to describe a memory, or to designate an object.

For every man invents himself unceasingly, though he does not know what the end will be. As soon as he stops inventing, he changes into a thing. Then he begins to repeat himself.

Now there are many different ways of repeating oneself. Some do because they have found a spiritual unity, which is ever being born again and from which all their acts flow. They have taken up their abode in an eternity where apparently nothing ever changes, but where, in reality, everything is always new. (For there is no true novelty other than the discovery, at every moment of time, of an eternity which delivers us from time.) The rest are content to go through certain motions over and over again, precisely because they have failed to find the inner spring of inspiration which would have turned their very repetitions into a perpetual spiritual resurrection.

Though it is true that we spend our lives discovering our essence and making it, it would appear that a moment comes when it is fully revealed and fixed. It is at this point that we see the individual either become a prisoner of certain emotions he has learned to feel and of certain actions he has learnt to perform—and he will remain their prisoner till death; or else he emerges free, wholly himself, and moves where he will across the infinity of the spiritual world into which he has just found his way, and where henceforward he will dwell.

At birth, my personal existence enters the immense universe, to enable my liberty to exert itself, and, so to say, to choose what I shall be. But how shall I have used this liberty? I shall not know the answer until death, which is the hour of every restitution, when my solitude is consummated, and when I cannot carry away with me anything but what I have given to myself.

Notes

1. cf. Genesis 3:17–19.
2. Matt. 6:31.

CHAPTER V

FEELING in all its forms, from physical sensation to high emotion, is our link with the universe, and so indispensable to us. Nevertheless it is only a means, in the economy of the spirit, to being. It must be "possessed," assimilated, and turned into food for the soul engaged in the task of self-creation. Neither pleasure nor pain are good or bad in themselves, but means to good or evil; the latter depend on the attitude the will takes to them.

The Role of the Sensibility

ⁿⁿ

1 *The word "sensible"* [1]

The French word *sensible* is sometimes used as a synonym of hypersensitive; it is then used to designate merely a certain weakness in the body in its contact with anything that agitates it and threatens to break it, a lack of courage and self-control. And it could be demonstrated that a person who is merely sensitive or merely emotional is not necessarily either discerning or tender-hearted, and that this is often a sign of weakness rather than of compassion, and of self-love rather than of love.

But *sensible* is such a noble word that it should be preserved from all usages which debase it; we should allow it to keep that ambiguousness which relates it both to the senses and to the sentiments, and never break the fragile bridge by which these are connected. It establishes a sort of equilibrium between them, and when this is destroyed, we are reduced to the words "sensual" and "sentimental," both of which have strongly pejorative overtones.

It is clear then that our sensibility is in constant danger, a danger which is seen to be all the greater when one realizes that, since it refers every event to the self, it is capable of exciting in the self all the impulses which stem from self-love, as well as all those which stem from charity.

Sensibility, moreover, must not be separated from the heart, although one finds plenty of it in the passive and highly impressionable type of person who is merely receptive, easily excited, and ever ready to take offense; while on the other hand the heart is also the seat of the impulses of the most virile individuals, those who are ever ready to give themselves, boldly and generously.

Nor, again, must sensibility be separated from love, even though certain people seem to have plenty of sensibility and little love. On the other hand sensibility acquires depth only if it proceeds from love, following it in all its movements and rising and falling with all its fluctuations.

2 A fragile equilibrium

The individual's sensibility joins him to the All, and yet the distinction between them is not abolished. It is the sign of their mutual presence to each other; it establishes the subtlest communication between them. It makes possible a whole range of stimuli and responses; these are inexhaustible; habit cannot dull them; they bind our life to reality with bonds so fast and so vital that, by comparison, knowledge seems abstract and pale.

It is our sensibility alone which reveals to us that we belong to the universe, and the point at which we are in contact with it. It is the living link between what has its origin in us and what proceeds from *it*. In its highest forms—as can be seen in joy and in love—it expresses a harmony between the active and the passive principles of the soul, between what we desire and what is given us.

It has often been remarked that, as life developed on the surface of the earth, the creatures which survived were not the strongest, the most violent and the most brutal—for the soil on which we walk today is their cemetery—but rather the frail creatures of feeling, with their thin, light bones, the Stone Age creatures, which first established a fragile equilibrium between their needs and the forces of Nature. They were responsive to every impulsion, whether coming from without them or from within, though incapable as yet of distinguishing between an idea, which is a product of the intelligence, and an instinctual urge; but their dawning consciousness seemed to foreshadow a later development, when the life of the body would be but a prelude to the life of the spirit, a stage at which physical life would support the spiritual, and to which one day it would be sacrificed.

3 The sensibility of the body

Sensibility presupposes a delicacy of the body, which reacts to the subtlest and most remote happenings outside it, enabling it to distinguish their finest differences—its delicate equilibrium ceaselessly broken and ceaselessly re-established. Occasionally indeed it is invaded by a sort of tumult, which the individual cannot dominate. Because of our sensibility, we cannot stand aloof from the world without; through our sensibility, the world acquires a sort of consubstantiality with us; our body is bound to it by mysterious fibers, so that no one of these can be touched without our whole being being affected.

I may well stand in awe and admiration before the fact that, thanks to my sensibility, my body is penetrated by my self; that it participates in my self-awareness; that it seems to be a perfect expression of the harmony or the discord reigning between the universe and my self. Sensibility is that property of the body by which I recognize it as belonging to me; this means that my body has already begun to be spiritualized. The revelation of its own existence which is vouchsafed to the body is so sharp that it is, in effect, the sign that the body has begun to disappear, as indeed happens at those moments of violent feeling when a man is on the verge of swooning away.

The fact that my sensibility is bound up so closely with my body and with everything that affects it, is at once a necessity which I must accept (since I cannot be bound to the universe in any other way), and a contradiction (since my sensibility is the essence of my innermost self, of that in me which can never be a spectacle for others, as my body is). Nevertheless, one can imagine a pure sensibility, in which the soul has ceased to suffer the influence of the body, having brought it into submission to itself. We would then respond to the body's subtlest impulses while remaining unaware of its existence. The distinction between the soul and the body would disappear: not that the body would have ceased to exist, but it would be restricted to its proper function, namely to be the faithful expression of the soul.

Sensibility is present throughout the whole range of the soul's activities, from the humblest, where she is still attached to the earth, to the most sublime, where the earth is lost to view. Furthermore, she must never renounce the task of fusing them into a unity. If she does, she will either succumb to a flood-tide of the senses in which her inner drive will be dissipated and finally exhausted, or else she will be consumed by a spiritual fire which burns itself out for lack of fuel. The joys of the earth are her concern; these she must unify, spiritualize, and bear with her up to heaven.

4 *The sensibility, echo of the will*

The power which things possess to act upon our sensibility establishes a communication between them and us, at once intimate and real: by comparison, the best efforts of the intellect seem futile and ineffectual. But we must not yield to this power. If we do, we soon become the slaves of things. Sooner or later the sensible charm fades, proving to be a promise which has not been kept, and an invitation which we have misunderstood. For the strange thing about feeling is that it appears at first sight to be an end in itself, a state in which the soul may come to rest, while in reality it is a stimulation whose purpose is to provoke the soul to act. Until this is accomplished, we possess nothing.

It is quite easy to awaken in someone else an interest keen enough to stimulate their sensibility. When we have done this, we have achieved a triumph with which we are often well satisfied, but of which we ought, in reality, to be ashamed. A poor sort of victory, to have succeeded in catching you unawares, and to have pushed my ascendancy over you to the point where you are beginning to surrender! The real problem is to penetrate to the point where your true strength lies, rather than to stop short where you are weakest; I must reach forward to the place in you where the spirit consents and the will decides, but consenting and willing in a way which commits them forever. Until that has been achieved there is nothing in our relationship that justifies my going to the trouble of opening my mouth or raising my little finger.

However, my sensibility has an undercurrent which remains virtually constant and unchanging; this, rather than the fluctuations to which it is normally subject, gives my life its quality and creates the atmosphere I breathe. It is always closely connected with a choice, which I make continuously in the depths of my being, and with the essential attitude I assume in relation to the universe. But the connection between them is very subtle; *amour-propre* constantly obscures it; to believe in it, an act of faith is called for, of a purity and a simplicity which are extremely rare. And yet it is only then that the sensibility plays its true role, carrying us into a spiritual world in which we discern the value of every act we may accomplish, and forcing us to the conviction that there is no heaven and no hell other than the heaven and the hell which we have the power within us to create for ourselves.

It is often said that in the reactions of the sensibility lies the secret core of the self,[2] but we have an inner abode which is deeper yet, and where the will is born. When we will, we go beyond what we are. And the sensibility should be the echo of what we will, reverberating in what we are.

Our sensibility reflects with extreme accuracy the successive changes which our intentions and desires undergo. If we seem often taken aback by the unexpected way things fall out, the reason is that the order of the universe is not determined by our desires. No undertaking of mine can be more than an experiment. There remains always an impassable gulf between what I achieve and what I had hoped, corresponding to the one which lies between my will and the reality on which it acts. The direction my will takes depends on me, and yet I forge my happiness or unhappiness by accident as it were, and as a result of the reactions I provoke in things; one can recognize here the operation of fixed laws infinitely transcending all the resources at my disposal.

5 Sensibility united to intelligence

We must not consider coldness, indifference, and a sort of suspicious detachment, to be the hallmarks of understanding; these are sometimes sufficient in themselves to build a wall around an analytical mind, and thus to isolate it from being and life. Sensibility is the seed-plot of attention: where attention is, there is sensibility also.

In the indifferent world around us, on every part of which the impartial sun sheds its rays, the sensibility picks out zones of interest which awaken our curiosity before ever we begin to direct our attention to them. The world becomes a spectacle for us only because we desire to achieve, in the world, the gratification of our desires. And so we must not believe that in order to contact reality in itself we must suppress our sensibility. The contrary is true: we should give it the freest possible rein, so as to enable it, so to say, to receive into itself the sum totality of reality.

Reality always makes contact with us first by touching our feelings, and what touches these is already one with us. But merely to be affected by something is not the same as to understand it: intelligence transcends all contacts. Its function is indeed to embrace what is beyond, to push back our horizons, giving scope to our capacity for thought and action beyond the limits of our body. But it is never wholly separated from the body. It may indeed be said that when we apply it to any object, it makes us feel its presence by a subtler touch; and yet we must add to this that, for the intelligence, feeling is but the first inkling of knowledge.

There are two opposite difficulties. One is to be able to fill the whole field of our intelligence with feeling; otherwise intelligence remains abstract, which is its commonest failing. The other, to avoid abandoning ourselves to the impulses of our sensibility without permitting our intelligence to enlighten them, in which case sensibility never leads us out beyond the domain of the body, and we often seem to be content that this should be so. But it is only at the point where they coincide that the idea takes flesh and becomes real, and that we win through to the awareness and the possession of what we are. The flood of life, which blinds us and carries us away if it is felt but not known, would become meaningless and alien to us if it could be known without being felt.

6 *A delicate balance*

Just as heat and light can be separated, and just as one can speak of a dark heat and a cold light, so intelligence and sensibility can act apart. But, in fact, in spiritual activity they always act together, mixing and marrying so intimately and so perfectly that they become indistinguishable. And, by a curious paradox, each endows the other with an awareness which it would lack if it acted alone.

For it is not enough to think; one must *feel* oneself thinking, and not rest content, as has been said, to *think* oneself thinking. If my thought could not excite my feeling and involve it in its own activity, my thought would not be properly speaking my own: my self could not claim responsibility for it, or feel its presence and its effects. But on the other hand, the union of a totally impersonal, limpid intelligence with a wholly personal, private sensibility creates a continual dialogue between the self and itself, and between the self and the universe.

There is such a thing as an intellectual feeling, if we may so express it, in which it seems that the real becomes present to us, and at the same time penetrates into our inner being.[3] When this happy union is achieved, life and truth become one.

For the most perfect kind of feeling is not the most violent, nor the most sudden in its reactions. It is like a pair of finely balanced scales, which do not jerk violently up and down, but register, steadily and slowly, the subtlest differences. A coarse sensibility varies only in intensity, but in its violent oscillations the body alone is involved. Such variations are not to be found in a finer sensibility, which transforms them into differences of quality. It never experiences the same state twice. At each successive moment, it registers the infinitely subtle nuances which distinguish the unrepeatable essence of every object, together with its mysterious relationship to our self. In the coarsest type of sensibility, the will is always caught off its guard, while in the finest, it is always consenting.

It is a fact worthy of note and rich in significance, that the gentlest, most exquisite sensibility is separated by a mere hair's breadth from the blindest and the most violent. Intelligence alone is capable of transfiguring feeling, encompassing it with light, and conferring upon it a perfect equilibrium. When the latter is disturbed, sensibility returns to something like delirium. Though it is feeling that gives birth and life to intelligence, it is intelligence which enlightens feeling and brings it peace.

And at the summit of consciousness, the spiritual light which is vouchsafed us is in exact proportion to our charity. It comes as a sort of response to our charity; it is, one might say, the charity which the world bestows upon us in its turn.

7 The humiliations of the sensibility

Our sensibility is essentially a capacity for suffering: we

speak of a sensitive spot when the least contact with that part of the body hurts. One can understand therefore that an increase of sensibility seems to be primarily an increase in our ability to suffer. How could it be otherwise, seeing that our sensibility constitutes the passive side of our nature, and that a soul which has been born into life, and which is seeking to put forth its powers, inevitably feels as a defeat every state which it is peremptorily forced to undergo? And so, every time our active powers are inhibited and held in check, our conscious self feels humiliated, and we suffer.

The French word *sensible* suggests something coming from without which affects us, and from the very first moment begins to tear us apart, breaking into the mysterious solitude of the self where each of its successive self-manifestations is prepared, sometimes provoking in us a violent reaction of defiance, at other times making its silent way through the soul, leaving an unseen crack behind. A living creature is always exposed to painful contacts, like an open wound.

There is, we may be sure, a close relationship between the pleasure and the suffering that the soul is capable of experiencing. And yet, paradoxically, it is perhaps more difficult to accept pleasure than pain. The former demands a more receptive heart, a trustfulness which is at once simpler, more total, and more rarely found. It follows that a man must be able to dominate his *amour-propre* if he is to accept the pleasure which comes his way, and give himself to it without reserve.

For *amour-propre* is often stronger than our desire for pleasure. Pleasure humiliates us by forcing our acceptance; the more we have pined for it, the more it costs us to give in to it. With suffering, the opposite occurs, for suffering provokes a reaction, an assertion of our independence, and when we accept it, it is as the result of an effort which makes and keeps us its master. In fact, the keenest, deepest, and most undeserved suffering produces in a man a sort of inner satisfaction, and feeds his self-love; the taste is bitter, but the diet is nourishing.

The day may come when mankind will need to re-learn the art of saying "yes" to pleasure, just as in former ages he had to learn to say "yes" to suffering; when, instead of feeding his vanity on the suffering he is required to undergo (while at the same time rebelling against it), he must learn to swallow his pride and to accept with gratitude the things which give him pleasure in spite of himself.

8   *The soul in torment*

Suffering is the mark of our finite nature. But it would be a serious mistake to see it as nothing but a pure negation, as certain optimists contend, thinking that by denying it they ennoble our humanity. It is not enough, even, to say with those philosophers who invented a distinction which has become classic, that it is a "privation" rather than a "negation"—the privation of a good which we desire, and which, on occasions, we enjoy. We know in our heart of hearts that it is a positive state of consciousness, more real, often, than pleasure, which is nearly always a superficial condition in comparison. For pleasure is an insubstantial thing; its reality can, in fact, be denied. It is as unstable as reputation, and even when it is keenest, it acts as a distraction. Suffering on the other hand fastens upon our real being firmly and tenaciously; it cuts through all the appearances behind which we hide, until it reaches the depths where the living self dwells, into the darkness of which the latter retreats, trying to make good its escape.

It drags from the self a double admission—that it suffers, and that it lives. This is the admission desired by the cruel child when tormenting an animal, the cruel tyrant when enjoying the spectacle of torture, the worldling ironically watching the eyes of his victim for signs of the wound he has inflicted. The joy which another's suffering gives us is the sign of our victory, not over a thing, but over the life of another being which has suddenly been laid bare, and is now in our power.

But just because suffering can only touch our finite being, it comes as a revelation to us of the reality of our individual and separate existence. We discover what we are the moment the world fails us, and what remains of ourselves when everything else is taken away. When the world is against us, we see, starkly, the tragic quality of our personal destiny. And the shooting pains of suffering seem intolerable just because they sever one by one the threads which formerly attached us, body and soul, to the immense universe. Nature was the first in the field, heaping every sort of suffering upon us, expert as she is in making us aware of the pitiful weakness of our body. When human perversity takes a hand, physical pain is drowned in a spiritual distress which seems irremediable. For the ultimate distress is spiritual; it is born of the spectacle of the will to evil which runs riot through the world, even though we are not always its target, and which lurks no less at the bottom of our own hearts, forcing all creatures to feed their sense of power on the suffering of others, and realizing thus a sort of hateful solidarity between them.

In suffering, contraries meet. When we suffer, our hold on being loosens, since all the ties which bind us to it are being severed one by one; we become like strips of flesh torn from the body whence it derives its life. But at the same time, in suffering we cling to being more tightly than ever, since every nerve that has not been broken is sensitized to the maximum. And so we cannot be surprised if, faced by this contradiction, the man who suffers should wish to escape from the world and life, and should seek in total insensibility the absolute solitude into which suffering is driving him.

9 *Suffering transfigured*

It is certainly wrong to consider suffering as the worst of all evils, and to make its eradication our supreme goal. It makes us aware of evil; it is not an evil in itself. And, by means of this awareness, it enables us to participate in being, and in the good.

There are sufferings which belong to the very essence of our condition; we may say that they are always present, although a certain blindness or hardness of heart often makes us forget them. The deepest natures keep them ever alive and present to themselves, and it is only thus that they find their way to the root of existence, and accept it in its wholeness, courageously, and open-eyed.

There are sufferings which belong to the dignity of our human existence. We cannot expect, we must not even wish, that they should ever disappear. No one doubts that it is a disgrace, and not a grace, to be unable to feel them. It may indeed be true that our deepest shame is our indifference in the presence of certain evils which our intelligence forces us to recognize for what they are.

We may be sure that the value of every individual is in proportion to the extent, the subtlety, and the depth of the sufferings of which he is capable, for it is suffering which gives him the most intimate communication with the world, and with himself. The extent, the subtlety, and the depth of all the joys he can ever know are in proportion to them. Who would renounce the joy in order to escape the suffering, and desire insensibility in their place?

So let us boldly assert that suffering must not only be endured, nor even accepted only, but that it must also be willed, for he who would dull it would dull the fine point of his soul. And it is not enough to say that we must will suffering in the same way as we will our destiny, or the order of the world, for it is suffering that deepens our consciousness, plowing it up, making it understanding and loving, scooping out a refuge in our souls into which the world may be welcomed. It refines to an extreme delicacy our every contact with the world.

But it is difficult to suffer with constancy and without murmuring, for suffering brings moral havoc in its train, engendering stupor, bitterness, the spirit of revolt in those who, incapable of welcoming it and passing beyond it, seek without success to throw it off. Since suffering penetrates to the secret of his most intimate life in the soul of a man, it awakens all the forces of self-love within him. Suffering never breeds the spirit of spontaneous generosity which often comes naturally to a happy man. Its virtue is of another kind. The real problem is not to find a way to anaesthetize suffering, since that could only be done at the expense of the total sensibility, in other words, of consciousness itself. The problem is how to transfigure it. And if all the suffering in the world offered us no better alternative than revolt or resignation, one might well despair of the value of the world. For suffering acquires meaning only when it nourishes the flame of our spiritual life.

My suffering is mine; it is not me. If the self gives way before it and becomes one with it, it succumbs. But there is another possibility—to remain detached from it without ceasing to feel it, and in so doing, to *possess* it. In this tension, the individual within us is at once present and transcended. Suffering becomes a sort of cauterization, which burns up the individual part of my nature, and forces me to consent to its annihilation.[4]

Notes

1. The French word *sensibilité* means "capacity for feeling"; it covers both the physical sensations and the emotions. The adjective *sensible* has the same connotation. It can be translated "sensible" only in such phrases as "I am sensible of the honor," or "a sensible difference"; it never has the meaning of "full of good sense." When applied to a person, it corresponds sometimes to the English "sensitive," sometimes to "emotional."

2. Fr. *notre intimité la plus secrète.*

3. Fr. *notre intimité.*

4. For a further treatment of the problem of suffering, cf. Louis Lavelle, *Le Mal et la Souffrance* (Plon, 1946).

CHAPTER VI

THERE IS a true indifference, which is not cynical egoism; it is the dethroning of self-love. Pity and gratitude are often expressions of weakness or *amour-propre*; charity penetrates to a region where these emotions are irrelevant. True indifference is the quality of the saint who, having transcended personal preferences, is able to penetrate to the essential nature of every person and thing, and so intuitively discern the action which each situation calls for.

The ability to forget is just as important as the ability to remember, but *amour-propre* stands in the way. Forgetting cannot be the result of effort, which is self-defeating; it comes from attention given to the present, which is our only contact with reality. This allows past injuries to slip away of themselves, into oblivion. Forgetting is one of the forms of renunciation; as with the others, it results in resurrection and rebirth.

Indifference and Forgetting

❧

1 *The two kinds of indifference*

In a celebrated witticism, Voltaire seems to give the perfect definition of cynical indifference: "At the end of the day nothing makes any difference any more, and at the end of all our days, nothing matters once again." But does this mean that nothing makes any difference to the universe, or that nothing matters to us? Who would dare to give it as his personal experience that nothing makes any difference to *him*? And if the argument is that nothing ever makes any difference to the universe, it remains true also that the universe's undeviating course[1] can either inspire us with admiration or confound us with despair.

In the same way, we are assured that everything is true, whatever is said. But it does not follow that everything one says has the same value: if that were so, every statement would indeed be nothing more than a matter of opinion. Only those who can think and live what they say know what they say when saying it. And though any statement can be defended, this proves nothing more than that the world contains an infinite number of individuals, each of whom can adopt a point of view which is such that he is willing to stake his own destiny and his own salvation upon it.

Indifference is either an abdication, a death of the spirit, when a man accepts everything that happens to him and at the same time refuses to imprint upon the world the mark of his action (or, in other words, to impose upon it an order of his own devising); or else it is the triumph of the spirit in a man who, without according any value to things in themselves, gives each an inner meaning which makes it, at a given place or time, the best of all.

There is, indeed, an indifference which is the consequence of self-love, and a sign of the hardness of men's hearts; but there is another kind of indifference which is a victory over self-love. A man who has attained it forgets his individual preferences; he discerns the absolute of each thing, and assigns it its proper place, its rank, and its incomparable privilege in the All which he is helping to maintain.

2 Indifference and discretion

Lack of sympathy in the presence of suffering may be due to the excessive softness of a character on which no durable impression can be made; or again to an extreme hardness, on which it is impossible to make any impression whatever; this last we often mistake for strength. But again it may be produced by extreme delicacy of feeling, that strong repugnance to exposing one's inner self, as much as to treating others without tact. And so it sometimes happens that a man who does not express everything in his heart, indeed struggles to prevent himself from doing so, and so passes beyond the facile sympathy to which others unashamedly give way, is then reproached with being unsympathetic.

What is often taken for unresponsiveness is sometimes in reality the effect of a certain intensity of love. A person may combine with this too much discretion to take note of feelings in another which, he esteems, concern him alone; and yet he may be experiencing the touch of that very love which makes us conscious of our divine origin. This discretion is the counterpart of the impulse by which a man carries love into the very center of the soul of another, where his spiritual destiny is working itself out. He pays no attention to some superficial attraction which he may exert upon another, and which he deems too personal; he disregards it as soon as it begins to make itself felt. He recognizes it for what it is—a passing impression which he would be ashamed to take too seriously, for he sees that it could only lead to a form of union with which he refuses to be satisfied, and which has no value unless it be transcended.

Again, it may be charity which restrains a man from expressions of sympathy, a charity into which enter respect for others, discretion, attention and love, and which on the surface looks like indifference. Such charity prevents us from expressing commiseration which might distress or overwhelm the other, as sometimes happens when people dispense indiscreet or oppressive concern. Charity itself demands that we should abstain from such. True charity liberates, in us and in the other, an activity which is not only deeper and more personal, but also truer and more efficacious; it passes beyond the appearance and reaches the essence. It raises each of the individuals to a higher plane, demanding of him the sacrifice of self; and this opens out before each a new world, in which self-love has ceased to be king.

Let no man reproach with indifference one who is, in fact, neither blind to others nor neglectful of them. It is often the mark of an over-plus of love. In such a case, a man is able to penetrate to the center of the most miserable life, and so far from melting into tears at the sight of his wretchedness and increasing his burden by his pity, go deeper, and, in so doing, begin to raise him up.

3 *Indifference and gratitude*

There is a certain indifference to acts of kindness which is due neither to hardness of heart nor to lovelessness; nor is it a sign that the person was expecting more than he received. Lack of gratitude, both in words and even in the heart, may, once again, be due to genuine sensitiveness. For often self-love lies

behind feelings of gratitude, while on the other hand the generous man who demands nothing in exchange for his own acts of
kindness, who is not even conscious of doing them, accepts
kindnesses done to him without thinking that he, specifically,
was their object, or that he, specifically, has been their benefi-
ciary. He finds it distasteful that he who gives should be ac-
counted meritorious, and that he who receives [should be] a
debtor. He rejects this idea of giving and receiving as too personal, realizing that the bond it creates is unduly sentimental. In
all simplicity he feels that it is natural that some should give and
others receive, or that the time, the circumstances, the situation
of the two persons and the nature of the gift should reverse the
relationship between them. He does not know which are most
privileged, those who give or those who receive.

This unconcern for self-interest, either one's own or others,
may be the other face of a man's keen awareness of the spiritual
order and its workings, and his joy in maintaining it. In this
case, a man has no eyes for what the individual in his separateness would cling to as a personal possession; he would have
him throw off all attachments, applying himself rather to a good
which is common to all, and of which each individual is the servant. He who is without self-love is drawn to other men only to
win for them the same freedom from self-love. His aim is to join
with them in an attempt to envelop the whole universe in one
common intention and one common desire.

4 *Indifference and disinterestedness*

Disinterestedness and indifference are closely allied. For the
disinterested man does not concern himself with things simply
in so far as they affect him personally; he gives to each the importance that belongs to it, and its value, so to say, in the absolute. With the result that being indifferent to himself, he perceives the differences between things; or again, that he can delight in everything because it never occurs to him to take delight
in himself.

The essence of indifference is that it compels us to advance without ever looking over our shoulder to calculate the distance we have travelled. Even in the activity of thought, it forbids us to stop short at any truth discovered in order to take possession of it and treat it as a permanent resting-place. For every success that we may achieve, in any field, is merely a triumph for the individual that we are—something from which we personally profit. But in the spiritual order, our goal is not profit but an act to be accomplished, the exercise of our capacities, not their increase, and the sacrifice of the self, which is also fulfillment of the self.

That is why we must adopt the rule of perfect indifference to anything which may happen to be our own, clinging to our liberty, which is never in greater danger than when we allow ourselves to be enslaved by success; for liberty's hardest task is not to acquire things but to find the strength to liberate us from all acquisitions.

All that is radically other than me cannot but be a matter of indifference to me. And so indifference is a defensive position to which we may retire in the battle with self-love. Indifference is the medicine for self-love, and should be brought into play only in situations in which self-love has been rearing its head. The purest expression of it, which is also the most exacting, is indifference to one's own feelings. It is the indifference of the will in relation to anything which may cause me pleasure or pain. The stronger the feelings, the more total must be the indifference. It then leaves our courage intact, whether Fortune crushes us, or whether she smiles.

To be indifferent to what happens to us, to every occasion and to every event, is to recognize the unique character of every occasion and every event, and so to make the perfect response. And this apparent indifference is at the same time an uninhibited self-giving, by means of which I am enabled to treat all the vicissitudes of fate as of equal significance, turning my eyes not on myself as I suffer them, but on God, who sends them.

5 *That spiritual indifference which is justice*

Philosophers say of the mind that it is indifferent to all things, which is precisely what enables it to comprehend all things and to receive all things into itself. The perfection with which it embraces every form is due to the fact that it is itself formless. Its weakness is its strength, the ability to reflect the contours of reality with perfect fidelity, precision, and pliability. And it is because it does not distort the essence of things that we are able to distinguish their essential differences.

There is a form of indifference which is holy. It consists in making no distinctions among the people who cross our path, bestowing on each our undivided presence, answering faithfully and exactly the appeal which each is making to us. Such is positive indifference, which is the contrary of the negative, for which it is often taken. Its sole law is that we should offer everyone the same luminous welcome. We must hold the scales even between them all, allowing no prejudice or predilection to tilt the beam. Then we become able to make the necessary subtle adjustments in our dealings with them, while at the same time giving each what he is hoping for, and asking for, and what he needs. The most perfect justice here becomes identical with the purest love; one cannot say whether it has abolished all preferences, or whether each individual has become the object of a preferential love.

We know that "to admit no respect of persons" is justice itself. This means, then, that we will apply to all the same rule without any exception, and without allowing our feelings to affect our judgement. It is to adopt the point of view of God himself, who looks upon all beings with single-minded impartiality. And this is the very opposite of the coldly indifferent look; it is the eye of love, which distinguishes the precise need of every individual, the word which will touch his heart, and the treatment he deserves.[2]

A man's indifference to circumstances results from the discovery of the fact that they are all incommensurate with the aspiration to the infinite which we bear in the deepest places of our soul, an aspiration which no finite object can satisfy. He puts all things in the world on the same plane, which is that of the world; he refuses to admit that there may be one among them to which an absolute privilege has been accorded, which might induce him to sacrifice any other to it. Nevertheless, by placing the spirit infinitely above all things, he becomes able to discern the subtlest differences between things, to adapt each to the conjuncture in which he happens to be, and to impart to each a perfection which is none other than that perfection with which, at every instant, the spirit comprehends it and turns it to account.

6 *The most insignificant events*

The virtue of indifference consists in putting great and small things on the same plane; it enables us to see that however small the event which is opening out before us, it is all-important for us. All depends on whether the spirit is present or absent in what takes place. The essence of being and of life is indivisible; it is present even in their most insignificant modes, and the problems remain unchanged however the scale is altered.

It is the same invisible activity which is able to transfigure the most banal contingency, and it is already wholly present in the least of our undertakings. Indeed, it alone gives them value and meaning, requiring us each time to take upon ourselves responsibility for our own destiny and for the destiny of the universe. For the All, which knows no division, is always wholly present without us and within, even in the most trifling occurrence. Every experience, the least no less than the greatest, raises all the basic questions.

The man who thinks he must inflate the scope of his activities, and dominate an ever wider scene, shows the emptiness of his soul. He is not concerned with the seriousness of his acts, but with the glitter of his reputation, unaware that glory may just as easily crown the most commonplace as the most outstanding achievement, according to whether or not they *appear* to be great. And yet it is clear, and it is moreover right, that the finest achievements are never seen by the crowd. Consequently, a man is bound to refrain from aspiring to an ever wider stage as soon as he realizes that this in itself is insufficient to make him great.

We should observe, further, that it is often easier to spiritualize small things than great ones, for in small matters, the intention clearly outweighs the matter, while the reverse is true of the great ones.

And finally, the present point in space and the present moment in time conceal sublime potentialities which raise small things above space and time, and which set free the spirit from all the images which would seduce it, and from the preoccupation with effects which would fragment it, leading to the discarnate act in all its purity, before a man has allowed himself to be enticed by the mirage of a conquest—either in space, which is exterior to him, or in a past or a future, which separate him from himself.

7 *The different forms of forgetting*

Like indifference, forgetting may be a virtue. There are, of course, memories which escape us when we would retain them, and others which fade, little by little, without our being aware of it. Others again remain with us, in spite of anything we can do, memories we cannot drive away however we may try.

Now it would seem that the future alone, which belongs to the order of the possible and not to that of the accomplished, depends on us, and that it is here alone that it is open to us to use, well or ill, the opportunities it offers. But we command the past too in a certain manner, fixed though it is, once and for all. For it is by an act which is still in the future that I can resuscitate it or leave it buried: up to a point, the past is still in my hands.

Forgetting is the mark of our weakness and our wretchedness, since it means that the individual is perpetually losing something of himself; but it is also the mark of our strength. It shows that our minds have the power to destroy comparable to their power to create, a power which is, in a sense, superior to the other. Further, it is a means of continual self-purification and rebirth. It gives us the presence of what is, by taking away from us the presence of what has ceased to be. It has an annihilating and liberating function which detaches us from every preoccupation which would impede us, enabling us to begin our lives all over again at every moment.

There is a forgetting that belongs to the flesh, which is purely negative, and which separates me from a past which I cannot bear to contemplate, and for which, together with its consequences, I refuse to take responsibility; it is as though I were trying, but always failing, to annihilate it by the sheer might of my blindness. And there is a spiritual forgetting, which is positive, by means of which I commit, as it were, the whole of my past to God, so as to put all my confidence in his present gift of grace. The first forgetting resembles death, and the second resurrection.

But if the ability to forget can be a strength, it sometimes happens that the ability not to forget proves stronger still, the cruelest of all when it produces resentment, and the sweetest and noblest when it takes the form of forgiveness.

8 *Forgetting is always incomplete*

In this life, memories never die. Each of them struggles to survive before disappearing, always leaving behind an obscure glimmer which subsists, even when the conscious mind pays it no attention. Its hidden presence is proved by a vague malaise which the conscious mind refuses to recognize.

Forgetting would seem to be always involuntary, even though the will often apparently desires it, or at least accepts it. Someone who has been offended says: "I will try to forget." One seeks to forget the painful past. But he who is trying to forget, in reality wishes to remember. In forgetting, the past must fall away of itself; when we seek by main force to tear ourselves away from it, it cleaves to us all the more.

The determination to forget is a self-regarding impulse; but in this case, self-love is fighting against itself, the self which still remembers. Wounded and humiliated as it is, it seeks to cure itself, but only succeeds in inflaming its wounds. For there is a mysterious complicity between the memory and the will: in the sort of half-light to which, by a sort of tacit agreement, the forgotten episode is consigned, the mind succeeds in remaining unconscious of a hated memory, but it is still lurking there. For our wills are divided, and, in the same act, my will can preserve the memory and thrust it out of consciousness.

9 *Forgetting and detachment*[3]

We must leave memory to its natural function, which is to enable us to respond in the present moment to the challenge of the present moment. As soon as it turns away from the action which demands its light, it harasses us with vain images or with debilitating remorse. And that is why one often tries harder to forget than to remember. The memory which comes to hand is nearly always sufficient for our needs; it is the attention concentrated on the self, and a self-love consumed by a masochistic passion for self-punishment, which refuse to be content with it. Then one can observe the will, hotly pursuing a past experience, and substituting for the present, which ought to be sufficient for it, a past, which it cannot change. In such cases the past is nothing but a crushing burden. It must be transfigured; and it becomes poetic when seen through the mists of a forgetting which cast a shroud about all its ghosts.

All the miseries of our daily life, all the mutual recriminations and resentments which come between the most closely united individuals, isolating them from each other, making them either hostile, or else patiently resigned and secretive (which is sometimes worse)—all this comes from the inability to forget the incessant pin-pricks which, time in time out, two people inflict upon each other by the mere fact of the duality which makes them different, in other words, which makes them to be. No memory is sufficient to give new strength to their union; on the contrary, it begins to crumble the moment they turn back to the past. On the other hand, it is always recreated afresh by an act in the present, in which the past is abolished, and the future left to take care of itself.

Forgetting should be a stripping bare of the soul.[4] Just as objects must disappear from sight before the memory can win through to their spiritualized and purified image, so this image must itself disappear if the soul is to be emptied of everything but the invisible power which gave it birth. Things must pass away, leaving nothing but their memory, but this memory must pass in its turn, so that nothing remains except a mark, but a mark which changes our whole life, together with the very appearance of the world as it opens out before us.

The progressive formation of our inner being resembles the work both of the painter and of the sculptor. The painter's art consists in the accumulation of successive touches of color. These innumerable individual touches outlast the movement of the artist's hand which applied them. In the same way, the soul seems to create itself, little by little, like a spiritual painting. But forgetting resembles sculpture, and its more abstract, severer procedure. It is the action of the sculptor's chisel, chipping fragments of marble away, that lays bare the form beneath. In the same way, the self must forget the events through which it has passed, together with the feelings it has experienced, and finally stand forth in its essential nudity. For without forgetting, purification and renunciation, forgiveness, and sleep, and death, are all inconceivable; it is always present in them all, though unable by itself to produce them. Forgetting is an essential element of all the noble forms of renunciation by means of which our being recollects itself,[5] in the solitude of its essence and its truth.

Notes

1. cf. Ch. IV, section 5.

2. Fr. *le traitement qu'il mérite.* But there is an old usage of *mériter* which would make these words mean: "the treatment to which he has a right."

3. Fr. *dépouillement* (lit. "stripping bare").

4. Fr. *dépouillement intérieur.*

5. Fr. *se recueille. Se recueillir:* "to concentrate one's thought on the life of the spirit in detachment from all material preoccupation."

CHAPTER VII

 EVERY vocation is unique. The difficulty lies not so much in fulfilling it as in discovering it. Vocation is life entirely free of *amour-propre*.

It is something which we create, but not arbitrarily or gratuitously; it is a genuine discovery of something we already are, and yet are not until we have made ourselves so. The discovery is an expression of our power of free choice, and yet it is only when we have discovered our vocation that we know true freedom. Until then our life is a determinism of the passions in which the strongest prevail: and yet vocation has a determinism of its own.

Vocation is true self-expression; and yet it only appears when a man realizes he cannot make himself his own end, and that he is nothing more than "the messenger, the agent and the instrument of a work which transcends him."

Destiny is not a set of exterior circumstances over which we have no control, for we influence creatively the circumstances in which we live out our lives. Nor is it composed of the events which excite in us the most violent feelings at the time, but of those which, often seemingly insignificant, are in fact turning-points, forcing us to choose, or refuse, our vocation.

Vocation is usually thought of as a task for which one has exceptional aptitudes. In reality, it is rather that which *makes* one's task uniquely one's own; it is the link between God, one's self, and the world.

Vocation and Destiny

❦

1 *Individuals are different*

To combine breadth and depth is a difficult task. Some people are totally preoccupied with the spectacle presented by the world which, if they are to be happy, must pass before their eyes in endless transformations. They have never done admiring its variety and its novelty. But their contact is solely with its surface: all they ask is that it should stimulate their curiosity and fill their minds with pictures; what they are really looking for is an escape from solitude.

Others remain rooted forever to the same spot, endlessly preoccupied with the same thoughts, endlessly turning over the same soil, that on which they were born and to which they remain permanently fixed. They turn their eyes away from the sun-lit, rain-soaked plain, seeking at their feet a subterranean spring from which to drink. How difficult it is, yet how desirable, to join breadth and depth, to follow every path from which life beckons, without ever moving away from the well-spring where life begins!

Some men are themselves springs from which life-giving waters continually flow; but the majority are canals which distribute riches they did not create. Then there are the nomads, and again, those who cultivate their own little plot.

Now "there are varieties of gifts, but the same Spirit. There are varieties of service, but the same Lord. There are many forms of work, but all of them, in all men, are the work of the same God."[1]

All receive the same light: they differ in the use to which they put it. Some are like white surfaces; they reflect it all around them; they are the pure in heart. Others resemble black surfaces; they bury it in the darkness of their souls as in a locked casket. Others again refract the light; they retain certain rays and reflect others, like surfaces of variegated color, whose sheen and tones change with the hours of the day; they are the sensitives. Others again are like transparent surfaces; the light in its totality passes into them and through them; no rays are held prisoner; they are the children of God. Some may be compared to mirrors, in which the whole of nature, together with the spectator looking into them, endlessly see themselves reflected; they are those who are nearest to us, and their mere presence is our judgement. And others are like prisms, in which the white light opens out into a miraculous rainbow; they are those who sing nature's glory in pictures and poems.

2 *The genius of the individual*

Every man is a genius in his own right, but it remains for him to discover the genius within him. It is precisely here that the difficulty lies; for the most part we envy other people's, seeking to rival them instead of exploiting our own resources. Yet it cannot be denied that whenever we are faithful to ourselves, we experience a joy and a certitude which excels all other pleasures; these hereafter seem insipid, their charm has fled.

The problem then is, how to discover our genius? If we seek to analyze it, it vanishes. Most men cannot help doubting its very existence when they see their lives slipping by in futility and tedium, or dissipated by distractions. It is true that even through the most mediocre of them there flashes from time to time a ray of hope; but this fades away the moment they seek to grasp it. Their daily tasks consistently obstruct and thwart the emergence of this elusive thing, which is never an idea which could be defined, any more than it is a charge of energy which could be harnessed.

The mere idea of a genius which is our very own always stimulates our self-love; it brings with it a sort of anxiety, but also a premonition of happiness, as strong as it is subtle. And yet our genius is at the opposite pole to our self-love, which consists of preoccupation with ourselves. Self-love sets the opinion of others above reality. So far from supporting our genius, it obstructs its free operation. Our genius appears at the precise moment when we repudiate all the preoccupations by which we are normally beset and distracted, and we are admitted into a spiritual kingdom which is discovered only when we have attained total disinterestedness; and this new-found world gives us what we could not give ourselves, something to which we now bear witness, and of which we are the interpreters, something which we no longer seek to accommodate to our personal ends.

The act of renouncing his self-love reveals a man's genius to himself. But the moment he relaxes his hold, it rears up again, glorying, and taking credit for the defeat which his genius has inflicted upon it.

It seems that consciousness has been given to us less that we might choose to be what we would like to be, than to discover what we already are. We are only truly free when the revelation has been vouchsafed to us of what we are of necessity. Until then, we think we are free, but, in reality, we are the sport of each isolated whim; we merely drift from one beginning to another, from one disillusionment to another, forever unsatisfied, a mere spectator of ourselves.

Can it be said that there is no worse slavery than to be imprisoned in one's essence? But the man who could argue thus is the living proof that he has not found his essence. The truth is that we have the incomparable privilege of seeking it, of coming to understand it, and of being faithful to it; failing which, it remains nothing, like a talent unused. There is a sense in which we can say that madness is essentially the attempt to escape from the law of one's being; it is the failure to understand and to love that self which we bear within us, and which it is for us not so much to know as to realize.

3 *From character to vocation*

The individual is his character, in the commonly accepted meaning of the word, but also in the strongest and noblest. The will is in constant conflict with it, but it is always the character that emerges, whether the will gives way or triumphs.

In character, the self is one with its manifestation. Character is the expression of the most permanent and the deepest disposition of a man, that in him which cannot be disguised. On my character depends my happiness, and the happiness of those about me. And yet the paradox is that my character is both me, and not me. It is more truly me than my will is me, because it is there before the will starts to act, and it is there when it has accomplished its act. It is not me because I did not will it, and because my will stands apart from it, acts upon it, seeks to control it, and to force it to serve its purposes.

For when we speak of our self, it is not our character that we mean, but a purely potential being, a pure liberty, as yet undetermined, and still uncommitted, which to each of us is the most precious thing in the world, and which, once discovered, gives us the purest joy. And when we commit it, we realize at once that no man is anything except in virtue of the truth or the error, the good or the evil, of which he is, in some sort, the bearer. This it is that each man has already found in himself, or is still seeking, or else is trying to avoid; it is not his individual nature, which is nothing to it but an obstacle or a vehicle; for his individual nature has no meaning, and indeed no existence, except in virtue of the value which it may assume, and in which it can enable us to participate.

Then only can one speak of vocation; but then it is clear that every vocation is spiritual; it is the discovery of our true essence—and our essence is one and the same thing as the act in which it is realized. One can say of every man that, at the moment of discovery, he "receives a new name, known to none but him who receives it."[2] Then each man enters into a greatness which is his alone. It is easy to see why this greatness must be at once something given, and something won.

4 Vocation, individual and national

Nations, like individuals, have a spiritual vocation, or none at all. Taking possession of the riches of the world by violence, or enslaving other nations, is not a vocation; but liberating them, giving them to themselves, enabling them to discover and to fulfill the vocation which is theirs, is. Here again, as always, we meet the blessed paradox that no one can realize himself except by co-operating in the realization of everyone else.

For there is but one spirit, in which every man, and even every nation, participates, by an act which is their own, according to the gifts which have been given them. It is for them to discover what they are, and to use them in a life of continual creation. No idea can be more salutary than that of the role they have to play in the formation of human consciousness, a role which none can play for them; or the thought that should it be left unplayed, the possibilities hidden within them will never see the light of day.

And yet we must refuse to admit in any crude or literal sense the over-simplified notion that human consciousness is a sort of vast, anonymous soul, which each individual and each nation expresses in a predestined way. The individual consciousness, and it alone, is a focus of light, an original center of responsibility. It is true that the genius of every people bears within itself the genius of all the individuals of which it is composed, of all those who come under the same influences, and whose individual wills are united in it. But the great ones invent, while the rest merely take the imprint; great men are always strangers in the midst of their own people; they are like men coming from a far country, bringing us some extraordinary revelation.

5 *The discovery of vocation*

There is a flood-tide within us on which we are borne; nevertheless, we are never quite certain of having abandoned ourselves to it unless it is we ourselves who set it flowing. And so my vocation is my response to the voice of my most intimate and secret being, when this response remains totally unaffected either by my will, or by the impressions made upon me by things without. It is at first nothing more than a possibility which is offered me; the original character of my spiritual life consists in making this possibility mine. Then it becomes my true essence.

One may miss one's vocation for lack of diligence in the search, or of courage in the realization. Again, one will not discover it if one forgets that every other man has his own, and that he too is called to discover it. Further, one will not discover it without sacrificing to it the habitual promptings of self-interest, and the objects of one's desire. There are occasions when we feel its presence most keenly precisely because we are being unfaithful to it.

It is extremely dangerous to imagine that our vocation is something remote and extraordinary, for it is, in fact, always familiar and close at hand, hidden from our sight beneath the commonest circumstances in which life has placed us. Each of us must recognize his own in the tasks which come his way, not despising them, or seeking some mysterious destiny which he will never find.

A vocation has no distinguishing mark; we are given no extraordinary sign that we are objects of election; our vocation remains invisible, although it transfigures the humblest tasks of our daily lives. Yet because it brings the sense of a correspondence between what we have to do and the talents we have been vouchsafed, it lightens our path and supports us on our way. When he finds it, each of us is born to the spiritual life, and ceases to feel isolated and useless. It does not absolve us from the obligation to decide and to act, as one might imagine; the contrary is true. It lays an immense burden on our shoulders, calling us to be ever ready to accept some new duty, to commit ourselves—never to stand idly by.

6 *The unavoidable choice*

Each of us would like to be able to embrace the whole universe in his mind's eye; this is possible, but only from a vantage point which is his alone. We do wrong if we seek to transcend the personal viewpoint in the hope of seeing things as they are in themselves; for then things elude us, ceasing to be related to our life; and they themselves become lifeless. It is not by cutting ourselves off from that part of reality in which we are that we can hope the better to grasp reality; rather it is by penetrating into it, with all the talents and resources we possess. For us, the presence of universal being coincides with the realization of our individual being; it doe not transcend it, nor does it exclude it.

Men are loath to commit themselves; whether prompted by caution or by ambition, they prefer to hold back and wait. So they let the crucial moment pass, coveting a higher destiny, or else because every decision they make closes their horizon, and separates them from the All they aspire to reach. And yet the fact that I am what I am, that opportunities are offered me to take or leave, and that a certain correspondence always exists between my freedom of choice and the event, all this forces me at every moment to make decisions one way or another. And the choices I make, so far from diminishing me, make me stronger by forcing me to impose a hierarchy upon my impulses. They unify these rather than divide them. They provide me with an approach to the All, an advance-post situated in the very heart of Being, which is worth infinitely more than the ideal which I had imagined, but which I refused to begin to realize, on the grounds that I must keep it pure.

No one can wait for the discovery of his destiny before beginning to act: there comes a moment when he must gamble, and
run the risk the gamble involves. And perhaps we should say
that the longing, the discovery, and the gamble, do not follow
one another in time, but take place together at every moment of
our lives. This is the drama of the present moment.

7 Fidelity

It is more difficult than one might think to be consistently
faithful to oneself. Sloth draws us out of the path, giving us over
to exterior forces; and *amour-propre*, which would convince us
that we are greater than we are, makes us strangers to ourselves.
True courage consists in recognizing our vocation and its
uniqueness, and remaining faithful to it, never yielding, whatever the obstacles. Obstacles are to be resisted, not submitted to;
but they have their purpose, for through them a vocation is
brought to birth: they promote its realization. Even temptations
are but tests and trials by which we are assayed.

Fidelity to oneself cannot be separated from time. I must preserve the memory of the past, even though my life makes a fresh
start at every moment. For even though life is an endless series
of new beginnings, must we therefore break with our past, constantly pursuing some new goal, denying all those which have
made us what we are? Or must we rather complete, and then
transcend, everything we have already accomplished, by continually returning to the timeless source of all possible acts and,
rather than conforming too rigorously to the detail of our reso-
lutions, re-shape them, put them to better use, increase their
fruit, even if we should sometimes lose sight of the original
memory, or transform it into a new resolve, as though it were
being constantly born again in endless transfigurations?

Faithfulness to oneself is the constant attempt to realize intention in act; and yet I must not forget that the act takes place at
another time, and that it has too much substance for any intention to envisage it in advance. Faithfulness to oneself is not an

austere, self-conscious consistency, the refusal ever to modify the original intention; the whole problem is to know how to modify it, whether it is a question of relinquishing the original goal, or of including it in an ever-widening view.

Faithfulness to oneself imparts a sort of nobility to the soul, a nobility which is both natural and spiritual; this is true self-awareness. Narcissus never achieved it. It is not the unswerving pursuit of a goal, or even consistency to one's past, but faithfulness, beyond every goal, and beyond the whole of one's past, to a design which no goal and no past can have fulfilled, and in the light of which a new future continually opens out before us. This we may call the design which God has for each of us, and which we may, indeed, never realize. In that case our life has failed; it has slipped by outside us as it were, and without our participation; it has never emerged from the world of appearances, and day by day and moment by moment it has passed into oblivion with them.

8 Destiny and vocation

The development of the plant is usually considered to be determined by the nature of the seed and the influence of its environment. If this were true of us, we would be enclosed in the net of fatality; we would have a destiny, but no vocation. Vocation presupposes acceptance by a free will, putting to use the gifts we have received, and the situation in which our life is placed. In the space between what we are by nature and the circumstances in which we find ourselves, free choice operates; between these two determinations, the inner and the outer, and as a result of their meeting, it finds room to move. It is the link between them; it demands of each arms against the other. It makes use of the impact of external events to control and discipline the potentialities of its own nature; with these potentialities, it takes possession of external events, or calls them into being.

The role of destiny would seem to be to bring us face to face with situations which, being free souls, we are then called upon to deal with. And yet this response is not purely internal and spiritual, as people sometimes imagine; it modifies our destiny ·itself. In fact, destiny is much more than merely a challenge coming from without: the will calls it into being as a field for its own activity. External events are the soul's opportunities; they are always related to its aspirations, its capacity, its courage, and its deserts.

Wisdom consists wholly in our ability to discover a certain relationship between what we purpose and what happens to us, though we will never know whether what happened to us was determined by what we willed, or whether what we willed was determined by what happened to us.

9 *Events and chance*

Our destiny is not composed of the series of occurrences which fill the span of our days, as is commonly believed. Great events may shatter us by their impact, but the violent feelings they arouse are merely an echo coming from our bodies. The mind may register the shock without being really involved in the event.

We sometimes magnify a past experience which, at the time, made an overwhelming impression on us. We whip up our imagination, we embroider on the memory, in order to make others feel, or to feel again ourselves, the same excitement as we experienced at the time. But we never succeed. Nothing proves this more clearly than the example of appalling war-time experiences. When peace comes, every soldier discovers the difference between the heat of the conflagration which passed over him and the ashes it has left behind, ashes which no effort of the imagination can fan into a flame.

An event may have the most extraordinary significance at the moment of its occurrence. It may leave us speechless, dumbfounded; nevertheless, up to this point it is a mere spectacle. It does not enter into our lives until we have passed judgement on

it, interpreted it, made it ours by the significance we give it (and
which we alone can know), for the drama of our inner life. And
it takes its place in our destiny when, and only when, it has become for us a challenge or an answer coming to us from the universe, a personal miracle, with a meaning for us alone, and
solely in its relation to us.

In the games of chance we become most clearly aware of a
destiny apparently determined from without, and facing the
player with events for which it would appear he was entirely
without responsibility; and yet each one comes to him as
though he had been aiming at it. This can be observed especially
in a run of good or bad luck. We must spiritualize chance itself.
We must not underestimate the deep-rooted feeling that comes
to us at times that we have managed to seize hold of chance, or
that we have allowed it to slip by; that we have lured it into our
grasp, or spurned it; that we have joyously let it bear us along,
or leave us behind, disconsolate. It is not true that there are, on
the one hand, the laws of chance over which we have no control
and, on the other hand, and entirely distinct from them, our intelligence and sensibility reacting to them. The human soul is an
agent also, in all occurrences: words such as *expectation, desire,*
and *hope* fail to suggest the reality and extent of its influence.

10 *Each destiny is unique*

One may wonder at the fact that a destiny may remain unrealized; but let us bear in mind that our destiny cannot be dis-
cerned until the game is over; we say that we have missed it
when it would appear that it has not coincided with our vocation.

There is no feeling more splendid, deeper, or stronger, than
that of the man who, down at the roots of his self-awareness,
finds the conviction that he is the sole inhabitant of the universe, with a unique and incomparable destiny before him; that
he cannot be the victim of any of the disasters which happen to

others, that he is the one who will come back from the war, that the death-bell will never toll for him. Now, we know with absolute certainty that all this is untrue. We know that in point of fact our fate will be the same as other men's, that every conceivable disaster may rain down upon us, that we may not come back from the war, and that one day we will surely die.

But all this is true of our body, and nothing but our body; it does not touch our awareness of our own inner being;[3] this is a world which no outer event can effect, a world into which a free, personal act gives us entry, and from which nothing can drive us, a world, in short, which is eternal.

The man who allowed this impression its full significance and its total presence, penetrating to its very source, would surely find liberation from the anxiety which is inseparable from the thought of his destiny. In the first place, he would catch a sort of glimpse of eternity, that is to say, of an inner being[4] which is unique, his very own and the only one he knows, but which at the same time cannot be separated from the inner being[4] of the All; and this latter is, by its very nature, imperishable. He would further become aware of the incontrovertible fact that what others know of him is a mere appearance, namely his body, just as what he knows of them is nothing but an appearance, which is theirs; and that bodies are under the law of all other appearances, namely that of corruption and change; while the inner being is not subject to these laws, but, by converting matter into spirit, gives a meaning to our own existence which illuminates with its own light everything that happens to us.

It is a great mistake to imagine that each of us is advancing in a straight line towards a remote and inaccessible goal. The truth is that each of us is circling round his own center, ceaselessly widening the arc he is describing in the totality of Being. From this it follows that the role of time is different from what we almost always imagine it to be. Time is not a forward-flowing, in which we must abandon what we leave behind, and are not sure of ever permanently acquiring anything whatever. Time enables us to trace a circle about ourselves, and to enclose in this circle an ever-widening area of the world, like a rose growing. It enables us to join together the perfect repose of our heart's heart from which all our acts proceed, and the perfection of movement of which is born ever new and richer activity. It is not the circular movement of those Greek philosophers who contend that no gain is ever permanent. For every soul, progress consists in the gradual coming to be of its own essence. It is a union of the finite and the infinite, compelling it to move forward towards a state of perfect maturity; there a man dies merely to bear fruit.

11 Every soul is "chosen"

Every man must act in the world as if he were conscious of having been chosen for a task which he alone can perform. From the moment of discovery and of his first consecration to it, he has the feeling that God is with him, watching over him. His soul is filled with confidence and joy; the sense of being lost vanishes; he is set free from doubt and anguish.[5] He is associated, now, with the work of creation; he is washed clean; he has no past; each morning he is born anew. He lives in the sense of wonder that he, puny creature and sinner that he is, has been called to an undertaking that is greater than he, a task for which he ever receives fresh strength, and ever feels fresh enthusiasm. Such is the mystery of vocation.

The sense of vocation fills the soul of a man, from the moment he sees and acknowledges his own, with incomparable joy. No longer is he lost in the universe, but rather occupies a place of election in it; he is both upheld by it, and upholds it; he discovers a correspondence between his needs and the help that is constantly vouchsafed him, between his desires and hopes, and the revelation that is granted him ever anew.

It is usually considered that vocation is a sort of correspondence between our gifts and our daily labors; in fact, it comes from beyond the former, and extends beyond the latter. It is the grace which penetrates them both; it unites them, and transcends them.

A man's vocation appears the moment he realizes that he cannot be to himself his own end, that he can be nothing more than the messenger, the instrument, and the agent of a work with which he is called to co-operate, and in which the destiny of the whole universe is involved.

Vocation is that which, in the exercise of our liberty, is by its very nature, irresistible. But, at the same time, it creates the personal and individual relationship between God and the soul which is the true object of faith, and without which our life has no meaning, and no contact with the absolute. It is the drop of blood which Pascal, in his anguish, prayed that Christ might have shed for him on the cross.

Notes

1. New English Bible, I Corinthians 12:4–6.

2. N.E.B., Revelation 2:17.

3. Fr. *intimité spirituelle*.

4. Fr. *intimité*.

5. *Anguish* has become, with the existentialists, almost a technical philosophical term. But cf. Job, 7:11 "in the anguish of my spirit."

CHAPTER VIII

EACH SELF is unique, and essentially alone; selfhood is therefore, in essence, a principle of separation. But Lavelle has shown that it is precisely this solitude which makes communication and communion possible. The barrier to these is narcissistic self-love, which he has shown to arise from a false conception of the nature of the self.

In the first six sections of this chapter, Lavelle deals with certain manifestations of self-love, in the individual and in society, which erect this barrier between men—the conflict over opinions, the hatred of differences (and especially of superiority), the mistrust of non-conformity.

He goes on to consider the phenomenon of pride, and the opposite attitudes of humility and simplicity.

He ends with two sections on avarice, a perversion of the spirit which uses the spiritual weapons of detachment and renunciation against the spirit itself. The spirit uses these weapons to fructify all potentials, material and spiritual, while the miser seeks, by the same self-discipline, material power only, and this forever unfructified.

The Pains of Separateness [1]

❧

1 *Amour-propre*

When *amour-propre* is in control, a man can be so pleased with himself that he takes pleasure even in his own wretchedness; with the result, that when he tries to cure himself, he makes himself worse.

I must not be preoccupied by the idea of myself as a unique and inimitable person, for this stimulates my *amour-propre*, an instinct which drives me to try to keep everything for myself, and to turn everything to my own use. A man acts and lives from the depths of his being when he assumes a free and generous attitude towards the self of which he is conscious, but which as a matter of fact he transcends, and to which, therefore, he ought never to allow himself to be enslaved. Narcissus remained forever its slave.

Amour-propre spoils our relations with others in countless ways. It breeds touchiness. We are afraid people will dislike us, then we imagine they do, when in fact they are not even thinking about us. Sometimes our suspicions bring about the very thing we fear: we create antipathy in someone who had no feelings for us either way, or who had even been quite ready to be our friend.

I see things that others do not see, while others see things I miss. The things which give people pleasure differ. All this gives rise to misunderstandings; and often we only avoid mutual jealousy at the price of mutual contempt.

At the root of every conflict are comparisons. In every situa-

tion there is a rich man and a poor man. It is difficult to say
which is the more repulsive, the contempt of the former, or the
envy of the latter.

2 *Opinion*

Nothing in the world is despised as much as opinions:
"That's a mere matter of opinion," people say, disparagingly.
Like Plato, we all contrast opinion with knowledge. And yet, at
the same time, our own opinions are what we set most store by,
merely because they are ours, because they reflect a personal
preference, because they are a function of our personality. We
claim the right to have, and to keep, our opinions. Everyone
clings to his own as the most precious expression of his ego.

But a man cannot derive unmixed satisfaction from his opinions: the very word is a recognition of weakness. He goes no
farther than to assert that the opinion is his; he does not always
claim that it is better than other people's; he has chosen it, and
yet it was appearances that determined his choice. And it is precisely when his conviction begins to weaken that he clings to it
in a sort of despair. This is the moment that he produces the
supreme argument: "At any rate, it's *my* opinion," committing
himself body and soul to its defense at the very moment when
his assurance has begun to waver.

It is said that the important thing is to respect all opinions
equally. But this is impossible, and contrary to reason, for in this
case they cancel each other out: to say that all opinions are of
equal value is to say that no opinion has any value, or that they
are *mere* opinions, all equally void of any clear vision of the
truth, expressing *nothing but* personal preferences or individual
fancies.

It is no way out to say that men are unequal in intelligence
but attain equality when they are perfectly sincere, for this is
far from true. There is no need, however, to go to the opposite
extreme and to contend that the sincerest opinion is often

stupid, and that it may be completely wrong, for there is always, perhaps, a modicum of truth in a sincere conviction. The difficulty is that no one can ever say how sincere his own conviction is; and there is no doubt that it never is entirely, so long as it remains a mere opinion. The sincerest men are those who are the least ready to be categorical.

Opinions struggle to prevail over others, like individuals. Esteem for the former implies esteem for the latter. They reflect all the fluctuations of their possessors' temperament and vanity; they lose their venom the moment we reach knowledge and take possession of it. Instead of comparing his opinion with other men's, the wise man, knowing its origin, drains out the heat which *amour-propre* engenders, and refuses to follow it into battle.

And so it is not other people's opinion that we should rate as of little importance, but rather our own. For it would appear, contrary to what one might think, that when a man undertakes the conversion of another to his opinion, it is a sign that he already feels a certain insecurity, and is trying to reassure himself and buttress up his conviction by obtaining someone else's support.

3 *The plumb-line*

Every considered opinion expresses a preference, and presupposes a value-judgement. But men have different standards for judging what is perfect and what is valuable. A good standard, it is said, ought to be as flexible as the architect's plumbline, capable of taking into account all the complexities and intricacies of reality. But standards are inevitably more or less rigid; to a greater or less extent, they fail to measure reality, precisely because they are standards. Furthermore, each of us applies different standards, because for each of us the ideal is different. Our standards are, of course, the sign that each of us participates in the absolute, and there can only be one absolute.

But every man participates in it in his own way and according to his own nature, and each battles with each of the others in the name of what he sees of it. And he thinks he is refusing to betray the truth, when in reality what he opposes in another is that participation with the absolute which by nature he cannot share.

From this it follows that disagreements are not due solely to the greater or less subtlety, penetration, or depth of men's minds; the very nature of absolute value always enters into the dispute, for each man is convinced of the truth of his own vision. And when men fight, it is not only for themselves, as is usually believed, but for that part of the absolute whose presence they feel within them; and these different visions set them all at loggerheads, though they ought to unite them.

Each of us is a unique and incomparable being, superior to every other in respect of everything belonging to his pure essence; in other words, in everything bodying forth in space and time his original relation with the Absolute. But what ought to humble us is the fact that for the very same reason, each of us is inferior to everyone else in the world—and this includes the humblest and the most miserable of men—in respect of certain things that have been vouchsafed to them, and which bear witness to the unique gifts which each possesses.

Blinded by *amour-propre*, we always tend to judge others by their inability to do something at which we think ourselves particularly adept, but in a domain which, in effect, is our own. We rarely think of estimating our own incapacities in *their* proper domain.

4 Hostility to non-conformers

One should not resent the hostility to which every individual is liable, and which increases in proportion to his greatness and his originality. This is not only a law of human society, but a fundamental law of Being itself. For every departure from uniformity, whether in the primitive undifferentiated mass, or in a social group where the gregarious instinct is still operative, threatens the cohesion of the All, and the equal place and the equal dignity of each individual which belongs to it. This provokes a spontaneous reaction, compensatory and destructive, the object of which is to restore the original equilibrium. It may be said that everything that serves to enhance one member tends to diminish others, but the argument is specious: the change may be in either direction, depending on the situation. But even so, one tendency prevails over all others, making for the obliteration of individual differences in the undifferentiated All.

From the moment of our birth, hostility and suspicion rise up about us. We must not be surprised. For we ourselves do not easily tolerate in others expressions of their individuality; we discern all too easily their pretentiousness, their flimsiness, their absurdity. But then, we have our own, which are different. These we cannot see, but they are all too visible to others.

The bitterest and profoundest antipathies are those which arise over the most trivial matters: two essences are suddenly laid bare, and an insoluble conflict is born. Reasons are always forthcoming, clear and convincing explanations, but in fact they disguise its real source. For these superficial rubs are not what matter, and even the most painful cease to count the moment two men strip off the masks they normally hide behind. Then it is that whatever one of them says or does, however innocuous, becomes for the other an occasion for hatred, and its justification. It sometimes happens that the very words and acts most calculated to lead to friendship and understanding provoke the most irreparable enmities and the keenest bitterness.

Life sometimes offers the amazing spectacle of a single word alienating two men, hitherto firm friends. Serious disagreements, open disputes, material interests in conflict had all been unable to do it. The reason is that the fatal word was *disinterested*. The man sought no personal advantage; he did not intend to give offense. The remark may have escaped him by pure chance, apparently innocent, insignificant. But that is precisely the point: it came from the depths. It expressed his essential being; it laid his essence bare.

5 *Criticizing greatness*

Since all greatness is relative, some men have no other means of increasing their stature than by belittling those around them. The great are their favorite target. Eternally negative judgements which, they think, place them above what they criticize, an inexhaustible flood of fault-finding whose purpose is to prove how exacting are their standards and how rich their imagination, and this may persuade us that we are in the presence of a grandiose edifice; in reality, it is a heap of ruins. These critics do not rise superior to what they destroy. Their soul is empty, big with wind, and wind alone. Nothing could fill their emptiness but those very discoveries which others have made, and of which they were incapable. But they prefer to annihilate these others, rather than appear obliged to seek nourishment from them.

Every criticism evaluates the critic, putting him above, below, or on a level with the object of his criticism. Some men take upon themselves the right to judge others without realizing that they are thereby passing judgement on themselves, and not always in the sense they had intended.

The greatest creations in art or literature are those which lie most open to criticism: they go so far and no further, just because they express the choice made by their creators, which was to go thus far, and to stop precisely there. It is also true that they are bearers of infinity, but as an unrealized, not a realized potentiality. Such works are a godsend to the critic. Forever seeking weaknesses, fallings short, they can be sure, here, of being right. But what do they offer us in exchange? A return to the undifferentiated nothingness[2] which should never have been disturbed? Or is it an opportunity to cooperate with an imperfect creation, and in so doing, to enrich it indefinitely, by revealing new aspects of being implicit in it, which the artist had left in the shadow? The greatest critics increase the stature of the works they criticize, the small men always diminish it.

But the spiteful man can be practically sure of his quarry, even when he attacks the supremely great, for he can count on producing a reaction of anger and wounded pride, which is humiliating to his victim, and his own justification.

6 *Hatred of the spiritually-minded*
No one realizes his life alone, but only through the mediation of others. I need the reassurance and the help of friends, but I need men's hatred too. It tests me, forces me to become aware of my limitations, to grow, to perform a work of ceaseless self-purification; it makes me more and more faithful to myself, protects me against all the temptations to take the easy way to "success"; it compels me to fall back on what is deepest, most secret and most spiritual in me, where those who hate me are powerless to hurt, where they meet no object into which to fix their claws, and nothing they can destroy. And the most spiritual men are also inevitably the most hated: for hatred is nothing but love enslaved, jealous of itself, and enraged by its own impotence. The fate of the righteous man in the Gospel story is ever there for us to see.

The most implacable hatred is reserved for those who have achieved a genuine, and not merely a feigned indifference to the things by which others set most store. It is specially virulent in those who possess these things, and are in a position to bestow them on others, for they fancy they are being slighted, and further, deprived of the sole source of influence available to them.

The smallest spiritual progress which we make isolates us from others. They recognize in us someone who has begun to be sufficient unto himself.

The world hates all those who are not of the world, namely those who do not belong to a closed society which is sufficient unto itself, but in which no one is sufficient unto himself alone, a society which only values a thing for its appearance and for the opinions of others which form about it. It hates all those who have access to another world, in which public opinion counts for nothing; for here every individual *is* sufficient unto himself. In this world, reality is interior and invisible, appearances melt away, public opinion has no weight. The world of the spirit lies beyond the world of matter; it can never become an object of observation, and yet in it alone we live. At the first glimpse of it we catch, every object fades and dissolves away, except in so far as it becomes a means or a sign.

7 *Pride and humility*

The greatest source of humility for truly spiritual men is the presence of the body, which, for the superficial, is the source of every form of vanity. I co-habit with a body; I must learn to recognize that it belongs to me, though most men think that it *is* me; I have to provide for its needs, bear with its infirmities, be willing that it should lay my soul bare to public gaze by what one might call an endless indiscretion; this, more than anything, forces me to humble myself. But true humility is a metaphysical attitude which is exceptionally rare. It is the utter abasement of my whole being to the earth, and it demands of me a supreme uplifting of my soul to God. For no one makes himself naught except to let God fill the void. And it was in God alone that total humility was once realized, which was the miracle of the voluntary Incarnation.

There is such a thing as false humility, which is in reality a form of pride. We despise everything others possess or value, silently congratulating ourselves on being above all that sort of thing, and yet on being uniquely humble. The humble man must not abase himself before God and then assume superiority over other men, using this abasement, which they, poor souls, are incapable of, as a weapon against them. Such a man demands more of others than he demands of himself. There is no attitude more difficult to maintain than that of true humility. from which *amour-propre* seeks no satisfaction by way of compensation.

Only humility begets gentleness; pride is always impatient and irritable. And to take pride in one's gentleness would destroy one's gentleness. But the gentle person does not think about himself enough to become irritated with others. And pride makes us so pleased with ourselves that all the gifts we receive leave us discontented, while humility, by making us dissatisfied with ourselves, enables us to take pleasure in the smallest gifts. And total humility makes us satisfied with the little that we are, however unworthy it may appear to us to be.

8 *Humility and esteem for others*

Only humility can keep us firmly planted on the soil in which we live and grow; when we are rooted there we fear no fall. We should not consider it a virtue: it only appears to be one because pride, which makes us the center of the world, inflating the little parcel of reality which we occupy until it fills infinity itself, is of all vices the most tenacious. Humility makes us take note of what we are not, and forces us to correct the estimate of our pride. But it does so to enable us to find our true measure.

For humility is not self-contempt, which is degrading, and which is almost always the sign of resentment directed against ourselves, and against the universe to which we belong. Self-contempt deprives us of all our resources, while humility establishes their limits, so that we may use them better.

Not that it is easy. One cannot see oneself as one sees others. If one is both judge and plaintiff, one cannot apply the common rule. When judging ourselves, we must fix our eyes on our duties; when judging others, on their rights. Mean souls admire nothing but their own achievements, and despise others'; the generous count their own for nothing and see in the achievements of others some gift which calls forth their praise, and in which they recognize a deficiency of their own. The former are exacting with others, the latter with themselves. In this case, humility, while still the opposite of pride, becomes a mark of spiritual aristocracy.

True humility consists in valuing others more than oneself, in taking note of what they have, and of what one lacks oneself. While most people seek to read others lessons, humility is the willingness to receive them. It creates the closest bonds between men; for though it is always within my power to reject what another forces upon me, or even what he offers me, it is by what I am humble enough to ask of him, or even to take from him without asking, that I bind myself to him.

9 *Be simple rather than humble*

"Humiliation" is an ambiguous word, but this reflects the ambiguity of life itself. It is equally true that the willingness to accept any humiliation without reacting is the sign of contemptible weakness, and that the ability to accept it without harboring bitterness or the desire for vengeance is the sign of the rarest courage. A humiliation accepted is not always the sign of lack of spirit; on the other hand the soul of a man who humbles himself unreservedly before God, but gives people to understand that he never humbles himself before another man, is sometimes the dwelling place of pride.

The individual must maintain a certain dignity amidst humiliations, otherwise he denies the presence within himself of a soul capable of a high spiritual destiny. At the same time, he must preserve the sense of his own essential wretchedness, which goes further than any insult could go, and this must make him ready not only to forgive the latter, but also to accept it willingly.

Humiliations almost always wound our *amour-propre* in some particularly sensitive spot. It is for us to cauterize the wound by curing ourselves of *amour-propre* precisely where it smarts.

However, humility can at best be no more than a momentary and provisional reaction of the will, to be resorted to when one is searching for remedies for self-love, vanity, or pride, just as one straightens a bent stick by bending it in the opposite direction. But one's object is a straight stick, and spiritual rectitude is the product of *simplicity*. The will must be undeviating, as straight as a die, but the soul must react simply and naturally to reality and to life, sensitive to their infinitely subtle complexities.

10 *Avarice, the intoxication of pure power*

Avarice, together with pride, is the essential vice of self-love. Avarice is distinct from cupidity, in that it is the longing to save money rather than to acquire it. The miser enjoys what he possesses, and will not gamble with it in order to make more.

The miser is a solitary man; he enjoys his wealth in secret; for he can neither show his pleasure nor share it, without endangering the wealth which is its source, because it would then cease to be exclusively his. He hates his relatives and his heirs, because he feels they have claims on him. He envisages all the possibilities which gold represents, but he realizes none of them, even in his imagination. He does not, as is often thought, picture to himself all the good things which he might buy; on the contrary, he thinks of them all as the greatest of evils, since they would be the end of the one thing he is capable of loving; to imagine them would be to contaminate the pleasure he derives from the power which he feels he wields over them.

Avarice is a vice of old age; it presupposes a long experience of life. A miser bends his efforts to accumulate the means to give himself all the pleasures which might fill his latter years, yet he scorns the pleasures themselves. It is the intoxication of power—unlimited power—but one which he never uses, because to do so would diminish or destroy it. It would be true to say that the miser enjoys a pure possibility, but a real, not imaginary possibility, since the gold is there in all its concreteness; the idea that he could convert it into an object he could enjoy gives him less pleasure than the knowledge that he will always refrain from doing so.

Avarice is a subtle vice, a perversion of the spirit rather than of the flesh. It is perhaps the essential perversion of the spirit, for it is the pleasure derived from the undetermined possibility of all pleasures—in short, a pure *idea*—and yet an idea which gives a more exquisite pleasure than the actual enjoyment of any object whatever. Avarice is inseparable from the idea of unlimited power, a power capable of indefinite increase, and yet which must be kept as a pure possibility, for to exercise this power would be to diminish it.

Money represents the imaginary satisfaction of all desires together, but the love of money blocks the satisfaction of every particular desire; the miser refuses even to envisage them. Avarice is the desire to be able to satisfy them, but to satisfy them never. It is, therefore, the only passion which does not become the slave of the object desired, not only, as is generally said, because the money which I do not spend can be increased indefinitely, but also because it represents all goods *en bloc*, while on the other hand the miser is not tempted to indulge in any of them even in thought, nor does he have to struggle against their allurements though pleasure is within his grasp.

The miser is the man of all men who needs money least: he is the ascetic who loves his asceticism. He wants money to be there but he hates using it. He is the most absurd of all creatures, but he is also the man whose enjoyment is the most detached— a joy strictly without content. Love of money has enabled him to triumph over all other desires. He has found that money, which makes their satisfaction possible, makes us superior to them, and that spending, in the act of gratifying them, puts us once again under their yoke.

The miser's joy is based, therefore, on an inner contradiction, but one which renders it particularly keen; he can have anything, but he rejects everything; he possesses all, and possesses nothing. It is within his power to transform a possible possession into a real one, but his delight is never to use his power. Such is the love of gold—a passion which can oust the love of pleasure, and which makes the miser endure every hardship, and little by little to become the enemy of pleasure; in the end he renounces it altogether, after having apparently pursued it. In the quest for the Rhine Gold, there is the mark of a spiritual perversion, a desperate struggle for the good things of the earth, the devotion of one's life and energies to the battle, with the failure ever to possess them; and, in the end, the possession of nothing but the effort made to acquire them.[3]

11 *Spiritual gold*

There is such a thing as spiritual avarice, corresponding to material avarice. In the spiritual life there are the savers and the spenders. There are some who continually pile up treasures they never use. They are afraid of losing everything, though here one *must* lose everything if one is to gain everything, and scorn the finite, which is ours alone, if the infinite, which belongs to all, is to open out before us.

Money provides us with a fairly exact figure of all spiritual goods, for though it is the contrary of them all, it obeys the same law. It is their contrary, since it stands for nothing more than what can be bought and sold, in other words for what belongs to the material order, and it provides us with a pleasure which we need merely passively to enjoy; while spiritual goods depend on an inner act, which we alone can perform, on the commitment of our whole being, which we alone can give. But at the same time, money is the purest of all the gifts of fortune. It can be accumulated without end, provided it remains untouched and unused. It includes all fortune's other gifts, for it represents the unlimited power to obtain them. One can understand why, of all the passions, avarice is the most violent, and also the most horrible, for its growth and development parallels the growth and development of the spirit, and it leads to a similar ascetic detachment, although at the same time it is only the universe of material things that it would make its own.

Although the miser's sole thought is for the morrow, which he seeks to master before it comes, it can be observed that he is trying to escape from time by protecting material possessions from time's destructive action, and by bringing into the present moment, where thought runs free, a pleasure which most men look for in the future, knowing that there only can it be realized. It is precisely here that the paradox of avarice lies: it endows money with characteristics which belong exclusively to the mind. But this is illogical, for it is only the mind that operates in the present, while money is that with which we exploit the future; and thought has attained its goal once an idea has been clearly defined, while money is meaningless unless one day it is converted into a pleasure enjoyed.

Avarice spiritualizes a man's activities, but without detaching them from matter, to which he remains even more closely enslaved than if he could bring himself to enjoy it.

The miser uses a procedure in the material order which is of the highest importance in the order of the spirit, for here it is a fact that potentialities are actions as yet not implemented; but he also debases it profoundly, for in the inner life no potentiality can be separated from its use, and use, so far from ruining it, strengthens it. The spirituality of the spiritual man consists, not in a sort of abstinence from every action which might diminish him, but in the disinterestedness and generosity which drive him constantly to act, without a thought at the moment of action for whether he stands to gain or to lose.

There exists a truly spiritual treasure, the other being merely its image, though the image ever entices us on, ever to disappoint us. Gold may engender avarice, through the terror inspired by the idea that money spent eventually runs out and disappears. But spiritual treasure only truly exists in its expenditure; spending actually creates it, and increases it indefinitely, whether the manner of spending be an operation of the mind, of the will, or of charity. But we can observe in ourselves a sort of instinctive materialism which leads us to consider that all the treasures of the spirit must be laid aside and kept for ourselves alone, as though they were liable to waste and corruption if shared; whereas true wisdom consists in regarding material wealth also as being indeed wealth, but only at the moment of spending, and that it too can be increased, and its nature changed—in other words, it can be spiritualized—by the good use to which we put it.

Notes

1. Fr. *Tourments de l'individu.*

2. Fr. *non-être*

3. In the medieval epic from which Wagner drew the story of *The Ring of the Nibelung*, the Rhine gold was a treasure coveted by a number of persons; in their efforts to gain possession of it, each of them brought about his own destruction.

CHAPTER IX

HAVING discussed the barriers men erect between themselves and others, Lavelle goes on to discuss the conditions which must be observed if the solitude of the individual is to be broken down.

Communion may be desired but not sought. However, presence to oneself and to others leads inevitably to the end of hate (both for oneself and for others) and to the beginning of communion. Service is essential, for though this usually means that one manifested self goes to the aid of another manifested self in some act in time, yet this act becomes the symbol of a deeper contact, based on the acceptance of one's own being and of others'; and this is love. Then giving and receiving are transformed, ceasing to be two acts and becoming one, which is both communion and mutual self-realization.

Communion

❧

1 *Two meanings of the word "common"*

Life has no meaning except for him who enters into a spiritual universe which is the same for all, discovering there his appointed place and the sign of his personal destiny. There he finds the *total presence*[1] in which all men have communion.[2] There he discovers too that the commonest things are the most beautiful—the air, the sky, the light, life. And it is the commonest feelings which bring the soul the purest joys.

But there is a type of life which is both ugly and common; this appears precisely when the individual refuses this ever-available communion; when he shuts himself within his own limits, with the express intention of remaining distinct from everybody else, revealing nothing of himself but his physical instincts and his egocentric impulses. Paradoxically, having lost contact with the common ground of all existence, and having kept it only with other separate individuals, he eventually patterns himself on them: he cannot of course surpass them all, but he will try at least not to be inferior in any respect whatever. This deceptive resemblance to the truly common life does not draw men together in the only way that this is possible; it consummates their separation. In this situation, men let their instincts or their vanity determine their actions; their spirit is silenced. Here is common existence in the most miserable sense of the word.

Common life is therefore either our activity brought to its perfection because we have discovered the spring which nourishes it; or it is life down-graded, which has ceased to determine itself, being passively borne along by exterior causes. True spiritual distinction consists in detaching oneself from things which are common in the second sense and discovering those which are common in the first.

One must therefore listen carefully when the word "common" is mentioned: people may refer to the things which can be won and possessed without effort, by imitating others; or on the other hand, to that rarest thing, which is also the most difficult to attain, because it demands of all individuals that they transcend themselves in a principle which is common to them all. And the risk one runs in a society where the majority rules is that the individuals which compose it should prefer those things which only become common by the universality of egoism, to those which can only become common when egoism is transcended.

2 *The separation which unites*

Separation and union are interdependent; they are reconciled in the living co-operation of two individuals in a common task which transcends each, and to which each contributes according to the measure of his genius.

They are complementary, not merely as two opposites are. Each is also a *means*, which must be put to the service of the other. He who is most perfectly an individual, and the most alone, is he who is capable of the most disinterested and purest communion. On the other hand communion is a delusion, destroying us rather than strengthening us, unless it brings us at the same time a keener sense of our separate existence.

This is because what separates us is the intervening space in which union is achieved. And men cannot unite until they have recognized and accepted their distinctive differences. When this happens, a man can reveal to another something in himself which he could not have found unaided. It is a mistake to imagine that I have to scan the horizon of my life in the hopes of finding others identical to myself, with identical thoughts and feelings; or that I should seek nothing in others but character traits similar to mine, and neglect that individual part of their natures which constitutes their essential being, by virtue of which they can say "I"; for this is in fact the precise point at which we meet, and which I must reach if my solitude is to be broken down.

If men could bring themselves to recognize the uniqueness and inimitability of each individual, their egoism and their jealousy would fade away, and a mutual admiration would develop; their instinct would be to hold out the hand of friendship, rather than to repulse the other man. For it is the uniqueness of every individual which expresses that share of the absolute which he bears about within him, if one may so express it, and because of which the destiny of the whole world will be influenced by his, however inconspicuous it may be. I think the exact opposite of what you think, but I also think that your thought is necessary, as is mine, to the order of the world, and that without it, mine would have no place or support; its *raison d'être* and its truth would be incomplete.

But man seeks ever to preserve himself intact, and consequently to defend his own type. He is suspicious of differences, as though his individual essence were being impugned, or himself attacked. Should he suspect in the difference the least sign of superiority, should it merely elude his comprehension or turn the eyes of others away from him, he at once feels disparaged, then abandoned, forgotten and rejected by a universe which he fears will finally swallow him up. The appearance of the "other than myself" is a vision of the universe subsisting without me, and shutting me out.

The differences between men are a test which is also a judgement. The weak and the egoistic take offense and would abolish them; the strong and the generous find in them ever greater joy and profit. They would have them increase rather than disappear. The discovery of their own limitations brings with it the sense of being supported by what transcends them; and so for them, all men become friends.

3 *My relationship with others is the same as my relationship with myself*

The feelings other men have for us are always an image of our own feelings for ourselves. Face to face with himself, each of us experiences more or less the same antipathy or irritation as he inspires in others.

This identity of our relationship with others and with our self is often too subtle to be recognized. And yet, he who relentlessly pursues another as though he would wipe him from the face of the earth, is often taking vengeance on the same person which he is conscious of within himself, and which he might have been.

"Mine" are all the natural impulses in me which delight or offend you, according to whether they awaken a similar or contrary response in you. But what is "mine" is not yet "me." The "I" is that in me which consents to these impulses, or which makes them serve its purposes; which defers or succumbs to them, or which resists and struggles against them. You may regret them out of the love you bear for me, just as I may disapprove of them once I consent to see myself as separate from them, and withhold my collusion with them. He who dislikes me may take pleasure in seeing me abandon myself to them. They belong to the world of nature of which I form a part, but where it is for me to choose; where nothing is imposed on me from without but I can change its significance, nothing that I cannot spiritualize and transfigure. And the essence of friendship is not to praise my nature, but to help me to take possession of it, with clear eyes and a quiet mind, so that I may make good use of it, modify it, and adapt it to my purposes.

4 *Seeking the good of others*

We are told that we ought to behave towards others as we would behave towards ourselves. But just as I ought to keep my eyes turned outwards upon the world and not inward on myself, because, being the spectator, I cannot be at the same time the spectacle, so likewise it is not for myself that I ought to act, but for others; I can never be the goal of my own activity, precisely because I am its author. This idea, once accepted, effects a double cure; it is a remedy for the pernicious effects of one's desire to know oneself which led Narcissus to destruction; and to egoism in action, which just as surely leads to death.

Now, by a blessed paradox, if I cease to observe myself in favor of those around me, I come to know myself without having attempted to do so. And likewise when I cease to pursue my own good in favor of another's, I find mine in the act. Every ray of light must lighten the world before being reflected back and enlightening me. The only act which enriches me is a disinterested act; only my sacrifices make me grow. And so the world is what it ought to be, its perfect unity is realized, only when, in a reciprocity which unites all men in one, each does for the others precisely what he refuses to do for himself. But then, the domination of desire being broken, he obtains much more than his desiring self could have expected or hoped for—not because others in their turn now act for him alone (for desire, for all its artfulness, cannot change its object), but because the act which is purged of the last traces of the pleasure-principle is the only one that ennobles and strengthens a man.

And yet it is said that the final word of morality is to love others as we love ourselves, and to do for them what we would do for ourselves: it would seem that that is the maximum that we can ask of ourselves, weak creatures that we are. But the reason is that this enlargement of the boundaries of egoism negates egoism and breaks it down. For it is equally true to say that he who truly loves, is also the only one into whose head the thought of loving himself never enters, and that love of others is the only pure love, which becomes, finally, the model for love of self, and which finally purifies it.

We know that the tree with the best essence is also the one which bears the finest fruits. If it is not to die, but to continue to bear fruit, they must part company at the end of the season; it is then that the latter are changed into nourishment for man and beast.

5 *On not trying to influence others*

It is not difficult to see that truth is an act, a living act, and that one only finds it by producing it in oneself, and encouraging others to produce it in themselves. It is proved by its results, the communication which it establishes between ourselves and the universe, and between ourselves and all other men in our apprehension of the same universe. And yet a deeper and more intimate communion than this is possible. Its failure to come to birth leaves us saddened; and yet it must never be sought for or pursued. It must be an effect, without ever having been an end.

For when trying to establish contact with others, there are frontiers which we must learn not to cross, those which hedge around our individual vocations. In their very diversity, these have a beauty and a perfection which we must recognize and respect. To try to force one's way across these frontiers is to wound the sensibility of the individual soul, and violate the unique and incomparable mystery of its being. Furthermore, it is labor lost. Futile quarrels are soon provoked. And then *amour-propre* may take a hand, engendering misunderstandings, resentment, bitterness.

But if it is a vain enterprise to pursue a communion which constantly eludes us, must we then rest content with the idea that communion is an exceptional relationship between two privileged individuals? On the contrary, there is no essential reason why each should not have it with all. Only, its nature is infinitely varied—as diverse as the individuals themselves, and the situation of each in relation to each of the others. The different lines of access are what we must learn to recognize. What would unite me to one would separate me from another. Only the greatest sensitiveness is capable of making the necessary distinctions. But to fail to make them is fatal. Here no rule can be prescribed, nor is sincerity in itself sufficient. Nor again are we further advanced by the dictum that we must show ourselves as we are; for we contain various selves, with various surfaces offering various points of contact with others, and different methods of approach. Cleverness counts for nothing here; truth alonҿ counts. The relations of a man with other men can become real there alone where certain possibilities are accepted. It is for us to discover what these are, and this can only be achieved after many unsuccessful attempts, many conflicts, and many failures. But nothing but perfection in his relationship with others enables a man to recognize his own essence, and to unite with them in the absolute.

6 *Discretion*

Influence on someone else is only possible on condition that one is not trying to influence him. Your desire to win me over to your point of view puts me on my guard, and stimulates opposition in me. Your thought is debased and corrupted, you are no longer single-minded, when you are thinking of your coming victory. A man influences another solely by what he is, not by what he is trying to do. The desire to insinuate himself into another mind in order to subject it to his own can only be prompted by *amour-propre*, and this in turn is to corrupt the purity of his spiritual insight. The latter is now contaminated by a temporal desire for triumph which automatically raises obstacles against itself; or he may use the expedient of pathetic appeals which only give rise to astonishment in the other, or to resistance, or indifference; these blind the other instead of enlightening him. To seek to persuade is to corrupt one's thought; one should seek rather to give it its perfect and most denuded definition, for therein lies its only possible triumph.

I begin to awaken another's interest only when he feels that I am entirely disinterested, and even, one might say, indifferent as to whether I convince him or not. He has the best chance of succeeding who withdraws farthest into the depths of his own essence, unconcerned as to whether others are watching, or understanding what he says. The charlatan is only interested in appearances; he gathers around him a group, but a group of bodies only. I must always show myself to another exactly as I am, in my peculiar strength and my own special equilibrium; I must not aspire to be a model for any other man; I must preserve the consciousness of my own destiny, with the corresponding thought that every other man has his, and that communion is possible the moment the idea of conquest has been abandoned.

Perfect humility is the essence of the matter, with the quiet assurance that our thoughts are our own affair, that we are responsible for them, and that our strength lies in them, even when they awaken no echo in others' minds. And further, humility bestows upon the soul its constant presence to itself, with the strong self-respect and vitality which go with rediscovered innocence. All this notably diminishes the value of the methods used by most of our contemporaries to influence others, to produce some visible effect, to acquire some exterior hold on them. All these methods fail, as is right and just. For the one thing that matters is not that I should act, but that I should be. For though it is true that I am only when I act, my action is nothing but a manifestation of what is in me; and I must expect not that it should be admired and imitated, which is of no importance, but that it should call other men to a creative work which is theirs and theirs alone, in the framework of a destiny which is common to us all.

And so we must observe much prudence in our relations with others, and not attempt to force an unwilling response, nor resent and seek to abolish the difference between us. By respecting this difference, by the discretion we use, by desiring, even, that the difference should be clearly manifest to all, we will find the path which will lead us one day to the common source of our double secret. Every man instinctively resists the influence which another attempts to wield over him, and he covers himself from eyes which would pierce and violate his inner being.[3] But he responds with total confidence and joy to one who would draw him towards an invisible presence, a presence from which he draws strength; for when another makes him aware of it, that presence ceases to be an illusion, a fiction, or a mere hope, and becomes the very presence of the living God, the ground of his individual existence, of the vocation to which he is called, and of his present solidarity with all men.

7 The light of charity

Of all the attitudes of the soul, charity is at once the simplest, and the most difficult to achieve. It is pure attention to the existence of another person. But charity is love, and love is never, as is too often believed, a rush of passion which blinds the spirit instead of bringing it light. When perfect spiritual communion exists between two persons, we say that there is an understanding between them; this is a summit beyond which it is impossible to go, and which love alone is capable of attaining. This state may not be recognized as such by those who have attained it; for there are no shadows there, it is pure light.

I cannot free myself from the desire to advise others, to change their ideas and improve their behavior, to make them agree with me; I cannot help desiring to make them feel and think as I do. All this is in part, doubtless, because I want to dominate them, and to make them the confirmation and the extension of myself. But it is also because I know that all individuals are really one, struggling to find the same truth and the same good.

And yet in every man there is also a desire for independence and separateness from all others, a refusal both to impose the law of his being upon them and to submit to theirs, a determination to defend the original quality of his vocation, rather than to enter with them into a common uniformity. However these two aspirations are really one. For no man discovers his own genius except by discovering the source of inspiration whence proceeds the proper genius of every other. Consequently, each will draw closer to others to the exact extent that he is faithful to himself.

8 *Bear ye one another's burdens*

Is it possible for a man to do the least good to another? Does not each man live in a solitary retreat, where no one ever enters? On the other hand, when he responds to another's initiative, can one truthfully say that his solitude has been broken down, or is it rather that a surface contact has been made, leaving the ultimate depths of their lives still separate? But even if it is only thus far that we can penetrate, is the effect not comforting or cruel, as the case may be? Is despair made keener for being discovered, or alleviated when shared?

"Bear ye one another's burdens, and so fulfill the law of Christ."[4] But, you will reply, are not my own burdens enough for me? Moreover, is it possible to bear another's? How could they ever become mine? Is not the desire to do so a mark of indiscretion rather than of generosity, of presumption rather than of consideration for the other? And yet, just as the knowing mind can only know the world and not itself, the responsibility which everyone thinks he assumes for himself is in reality the responsibility which he assumes, in himself, for the world. My own misfortunes I merely suffer of necessity; egoism is sufficient to ensure that I will do so. But for the misfortunes of another, I need an act of liberty and an act of love if I am ever to take them upon myself.

It has been said that the verb "to serve" is the noblest word in the language, and this is because it emphasizes the fact that each of us is subordinated to a good whose essential quality is ever to transcend the individual. And when we serve another, we force ourselves to go beyond our own frontiers and seek the goal of our action outside them. Then we co-operate with the work of creation, instead of remaining in the world of created things, or merely turning things already created to our own use.

9 *Giving and receiving*

It is said that no one can receive anything that he is not capable of giving, and that in order to be able to receive a gift, one must be capable of giving it.

And yet the honor we pay God does not consist of giving anything to Him, but of showing ourselves worthy of receiving His gifts. And if the good man is not honored by the evil man, it is because he is incapable of receiving anything from him.

Now the greatest good that we can do to other men is not the gift of a treasure of our own, but the revelation of something which was theirs already. For no one can receive any good thing which is not of his nature. It follows that he can only receive himself as a gift. Every gift one receives is the discovery of a power one already possessed without suspecting it. But as soon as it is revealed to us, it appears as more intimately our own than everything we previously thought we had.

And if the function of consciousness is to enable us to penetrate into a presence which transcends us, it is understandable that the one who is conscious of the good must be the one who receives it, not the one who does it. For he who does it needs only to act according to what he is already, while he who receives it finds his life enriched by a potentiality which he bore within himself, but which he did not exercise before he met the other man.

That being so, if there is nothing more sterile than a gift rejected, it may be said that he who receives a gift is the giver, for it is he who gives it its efficacy and its virtue.

10 *Recognition of greatness*

It is certain that no man can create his own genius; he is doing his all when he discovers it, and remains faithful to it. And he cannot achieve this alone. The greatest men need the reassurance that comes from the response or the secret sympathy of certain quite simple people whom destiny places in their path, and who are sufficient to console them for the ignorance and contempt of the majority.

For the value of a man never resides in what he is, but in a truth whose presence he recognizes in himself, and whose interpreter he is. And if he is not to feel threatened by doubt or despair, he needs must have the experience, if only for a brief moment, that the light he has received can be shared. The mark of greatness is a man's ability to have created an inner void within himself, the perfect silence of the individual, when self-love and the body are stilled, a silence in which all men hear the same voice bringing them a common revelation. And events of great moment also never fail to produce this silence.

The purest conscience is always the most transparent. It is in an abdication of oneself in which all his potentialities appear to melt away that the individual realizes himself, and that there is born in him the inner confidence which enables him to grow and to become fully himself. And it is when the attention to the object is the most docile and the most faithful that our acts are most efficacious and most our own.

There is therefore no such thing as the greatness of an individual as such; at least, his greatness can always be contested. One can even say that in one sense there is no other greatness than that which is recognized, or which may be so, and this often leads men to mistake it, or to judge it by popular applause. But we find within ourselves other, secret, intimations of greatness, inklings which kindle our aspirations and fulfill them at one and the same time; which sow our hearts with the best and most fruitful seeds; which break through the frontiers of our solitude and make us for a moment co-extensive with the universe.

Thus it is true to say that the greatest men are great not by virtue of what they give us, but in virtue of the way we respond to their gifts. In a sense they owe their greatness to us. It comprises nothing more than those same riches which we receive from them as soon as we become capable of recognizing their origin, or, in other words, of giving them back to them.

11 *Spiritual affinities*

The most elusive center of our vocation does not lie in the

choice of a task for which we seem specially made, for this will merely determine the influence we may have on things. It lies in the choice of our friends, those whose company gives savor to life, those who understand us and help us, with whom we can live in uninterrupted familiarity, those who never cramp our genius by suspicion or hostility, but support it and enable it to unfold.

The ability to recognize kindred spirits without sacrificing one's integrity to them, is the secret of strength, success, and happiness. The writer no less than other men needs a sympathetic circle of readers, if he is to develop confidence in himself and his work grow to maturity. Some writers may have missed their destiny because they failed to find, or to be able to create or to recognize such a circle, or again, because they had been mistaken about it. Just as the author needs a public which understands him and supports him (and often if his field of vision is narrow, their devotion will be particularly intense), just so every man needs a favorable milieu, like the soil without which no seed can bear fruit. But it would be a mistake to think that this milieu is given to us, and that our part is merely to accept it. Like every other event in our lives, it is a meeting-place of chance and free-will.

But we must be prudent; for all those about us, all those we meet along the way are, for us, opportunities and challenges. We have no right to reject them. And so what we are left with is less the choice of the people among whom we will live, than the discovery of the precise point of contact between their destiny and ours which will lead to mutual enrichment rather than to separation or enmity.

12 Predestined friendships

There is no one who does not yearn to find another soul, similar to his own, with whom he will feel united in thought and in the pursuit of the same goals. Reflection shows that it is in this community of desire that the true foundation of love

resides, much more than in the mutual search for self with
which it is too often confused, and which is in fact the perversion of love. Love always reaches out beyond the lovers towards an object to which they both aspire, and in which they
find communion. Although this object is universal, and it is for
this reason that we are obliged to love all created beings (just as
intelligence is universal also, whence our obligation to think everything that is), it is understandable that for each man there
should be one soul set apart to whom it is right that he should
turn, just as his mind dwells with special love on some favorite
idea, which is for him the gateway to the whole of truth.

There dwells in me a capacity for friendship which is ever
ready to be realized, and until experience disillusions me, I cannot understand why every human face should not be the face of
a friend. But this capacity can only be exercised by being bestowed on some individual. For I am myself a unique and individual being; my presence to myself is an experience which always occurs in time, in space, and in the flesh, and my capacity
for friendship is the same. It is still a mere possibility so long as
it is moving freely from one to another: sooner or later it must
come to rest. I need some one who, like myself, has a name, who
is alone as I myself am alone, and whose inner being goes from
him to me alone: it would be contrary to his nature too if he
bestowed it on all alike.

Every man thinks that one day he will find another man capable of understanding him, or in other words of being one
with him in desire. Now identical desires seem fated to alienate
men in the animal part of their nature, they become enemies
who would tear each other to pieces and slay each other; and
yet it draws them together so closely in the spiritual part that
they become friends, which is to say no less than that each one
becomes indeed the soul of the other.

A friend is he in whose presence we hold nothing back; we
show ourselves as we are; there is no difference between what
we are and the impression we wish to create. And in him also

there is abolished the difference, characteristic of our relations with all other men, between the within, which is only real for us, and the without, which is the appearance we offer to the world. But a friend is also he in whose presence we cease to be anything at all, and we can, without fear of humiliation, leave the question both of what we want, and what we are worth, in total indetermination. A friend is he in whose presence we can try out unashamed all the potentialities of our inner life.

13 *A glimpse of Paradise*

There is a moment when a spiritual communion begins with another person, which changes all the feelings we have had for him till then; then we forget that they could ever have existed without him. This spiritual communion only comes into being with the discovery of a world in which each shows the other what he was already on the point of seeing unaided; here every truth is bathed in an inner light which converts it into beauty; here every thing that is seems to melt into a desire which is no sooner born than fulfilled.

Nothing is rarer than this communion; most often it only appears in flashes, either with those whom we are seeing for the first time, or with those whom we know best. Almost always it comes as a fleeting impression; we cannot hold it fast, or recapture it at will. For it carries us out of the material world where the will is powerless to lay a hand upon it or to bid it stay. It is a spiritual paradise, whose door never opens more than a chink.

All those relationships we have with others—based on justice, for instance, or confidence, or sympathy—all these have meaning only if they prefigure it, herald it, and begin to lead us in this direction. They should make us seek it, even though success is not assured. So long as they fail to develop into this deeper thing, they remain exposed to every peril. For when two people first meet, it is as strangers who, as soon as they begin to know each other, are amazed at finding each other so different. When individuality asserts itself, its first effect is always to divide us. It is only later that a certain understanding is born, together with consideration for each other, the sense of certain limits to be observed—limits whose purpose is to protect in each an inviolable retreat—sometimes a mutual complicity between the two which increases their separation from everyone else; and finally, in the most fortunate cases, a mysterious union which adds a new dimension to the life of each, strengthening it and increasing its substance.

Although there exists in all human relationships a reflection and indeed a foretaste of true spiritual communion, they are all poor substitutes, and sometimes they even prevent it from coming to be. For true communion is far removed from the kind of attachment which chance or common desires create between two individuals, and which may be more or less strong and more or less satisfying. It begins only when two people become conscious of a presence which they are content to explore, and into which they enter by a mutual mediation.

Two souls can draw together only if they inhabit a single spiritual country. To discover another spirit is to discover other eyes meeting our own in one and the same light. Then it may be that we find a communion so pure that it seems purged of all matter, and as soon as the analytic mind discovers some, it becomes slightly less perfect.

Notes

1. *La Présence Totale* is the title of a work by Lavelle in which he had recently resumed his philosophy (Aubier, 1934).

2. Fr. *communier*, to commune, or to be in spiritual union. The French word contains, and so continues, the idea of the "common," the implications of which Lavelle is discussing.

3. Fr. *intimité*

4. Galatians 6:2.

CHAPTER X

In order that the Pure Act may be realized in us, or (which is the same thing) that I may "take possession of that parcel of being which it is my destiny to incarnate," peace in the soul is necessary. Hence it is essential to be released from worries, distractions, haste, self-doubt, quarrels.

A fact to remember when combatting self-doubt: our understanding and our resources are always sufficient for every present duty.

Gentleness, docility with oneself and with others, with suffering even, are the conditions necessary for participation, which is more complex, more creative, and more selfless than the proud detachment of the Stoics, and their contempt for the things of this world.

Gentleness and patience alone make truth and understanding possible—the understanding of Reality, in whose presence we are now, as truly as we will ever be, in this life or any other.

The Tranquil Heart

❧

1 The soul at peace

Inner tranquility is always the companion of solitude, and of the free activity of the spirit. It is incompatible with the tactlessness of the busybody who trespasses on another's task, prevents him from accomplishing it, and neglects his own. It is destroyed the moment I begin comparing myself with another, or when I leave my own domain for his, seeking to take his place or to triumph over him.

We must not despise the egoism of those who declare that even if the whole world fell to ruins, they would remain unmoved. For it is of little import if our body perishes, and the earth and the heavens with it, provided that our soul remains to the end mistress of herself, and faithful to herself. On the other hand, the fairest gifts of the body, of the earth, and of the heavens, when taken in the wrong way, become the worst of perils, corrupting the soul and making it unfaithful to itself.

Peace comes when we abstain from murmuring and from violence; but it is an active peace, for it gives us the strength to bear all the trials which come to us, and to love them as part and parcel of our destiny. It is never the result of spiritual inertia, nor is it a grace which we receive ready-made. It must be created by a spiritual operation of the purest sort, which dominates time and remains unmoved by events, makes us sensitive to others without weakness, converts confusion into light, irresolution into action, and every emotion into love.

Peace of mind comes when we ignore the importunate trifles

that bombard our senses like passing flies which our eyes persist in following.

We must avoid all obsessive preoccupations, and this, not in order to evade the serious challenges of life, but rather in order to see them clearly. For every particular preoccupation is a distraction, which means that of them all, there is only one that is worthy of our attention, namely that we should respond promptly to the exigencies of the moment.

The great and the strong are always immersed in what they are doing. The others are constantly distracted and preoccupied.

In any enterprise, the man in command should not be preoccupied, any more than the humble laborer chained to his work, to whom no one pays any attention, though everyone enjoys the fruits of his labor. How infinitely to be admired was the general whose country was invaded, his army broken, and who held in his hands the destiny of civilization and of the world, but who would say: "I am always occupied, but never preoccupied!"

One may fear that a soul at peace will ultimately fall into a state resembling sleep, and it is a fact that the thinking and loving mind can sink into a drowsy state, like the body. But even so, this state is compatible with an obscure and subtle kind of action; and, like physical sleep, it brings order out of chaos, and healing and regeneration to all the faculties. But true inner peace coincides with perfect liberty of the spirit, the liberty which enables us to perform every act lying within our powers, the liberty which endows us with a sort of spiritual agility. And this is only possible through detachment from all preoccupations, together with purity of heart,[1] and the gradual abatement of *amour-propre*.

No man is entirely free of the inclination to evil: we ought not to allow the fact to distress us unduly. It is sufficient to remind ourselves that such is our human condition, and that we also have a will to good, which is aware of the other will, which is superior to it, and which, even though it is sometimes defeated, does not identify with it.

2 Without haste

There is a point at which all the fluctuations of emotion and passion come to rest in a supreme equilibrium. Here the most extreme oscillations of feeling are not destroyed, but fused into a calm and harmonious self-possession, which is a single act of understanding and love.

Inner calm is the secret of strength and happiness. There is no nobility of soul that is not deliberate, and no perfection without immobility. By these signs one recognizes a force which influences others merely by its presence. For such a man, effort and action are unnecessary; they would merely do violence to his essence, and destroy his pure and tranquil self-possession. His spirit dwells above the world of matter, although matter is obedient to it. It has no conscious goals, as though every goal, being exterior to it, threatened to enslave it.

We must never be in a hurry, never hasty, like those slavish souls whose restless appetites distort their faces, proving that they have found nothing in themselves that is truly theirs— their one desire to get away from themselves, their one fear that of reaching their destination too late. But to what purpose all their haste? All the particular goals which they pursue so feverishly are similar to the objects which they already hold in their hands; it is unlikely that they will find in them anything new. For they are contained in the All, whose presence has been given them already.

Then why this haste? We will reach home sooner or later. We are there already. The problem is to enjoy what we have, rather than to acquire what we have not—some other thing, which we will not be able to enjoy once we have it. For the end is never attained, since we always project it into an ever-receding future. We must learn to abandon the idea of a never-ending chase: we will never reach our destination; we merely postpone living, and thereby never live.

Life breaks the surface of reality and emerges at the present moment; we must not hold our gaze fixed on a future which, when it comes, will be merely another present. The unhappy man is he who is forever thinking back into the past or forward into the future; the happy man does not try to escape from the present, but rather to penetrate within it and to take possession of it. Almost always we ask of the future to bring us a happiness which, if it came, we would have to enjoy in another present; but this is to see the problem the wrong way round. For it is out of the present which we have already, and from the way we make use of it, without turning our eyes to right or left, that will emerge the only happy future we will ever have.

3 Our resources are sufficient for our needs

The whole art of living consists in preventing our intermittent good impulses from going to waste and withering away. We must take hold of them, set them to work, and make them bear fruit. The essential sin is, without any possible doubt, the sin of negligence.

We always have enough light, if we will but accept it, to discern the best thing to do. Waiting for further light is an excuse for evading action. The search for a universal rule, applicable to all particular cases, in order to apply it to the case in hand, is something like willful blindness. Again, we would know the remote effects of what we do, though these do not depend on us. The growing seed does not know whether the fruit will ripen.

On this earth on which we are called to live, our knowledge is proportionate to our needs. Everything we have done will have its necessary effects in this world and in eternity, but it is not for us to foresee them, or to fear them. In fact, they are not our concern; for they are not the product of our will but of the order of the world. And we must accept the fact that we live in a world which transcends us infinitely, and that everything which originates with us will none the less end without us.

Life is lived in an atmosphere made up of popular prejudices; it is the very air we breathe. This the sole source of any equilibrium we may ever attain, and any effectiveness we may achieve.

One needs courage, no doubt, to sing the praise of prejudices. He who accepts them changes their significance, while he who gave them this name had no other idea than to cut himself free of them. Lammenais[2] said long since that to cut oneself off from popular prejudices is to cut oneself off from human society, and from happiness, hope, virtue, and immortality. It is certainly easier to discard prejudices than to make them our own, and to understand their real significance.

4 *What depends on us and what does not*

The Stoics claimed that happiness depends on accurately distinguishing between the things which depend on us and those which do not. Govern the former by reason, and ignore the latter—this was their principle of supreme wisdom, to the practice of which our will should be unceasingly applied.

But hiding behind this apparent humility there is the spirit of sovereign pride and contempt, contempt for all those things which do not depend on us but of which our life is nevertheless composed, and with which it is inextricably entwined. It is impossible to assert that we can remain indifferent to them, or that we exert no influence upon them, even distantly or indirectly. Such total resignation looks as though human weakness were taking vengeance on destiny, and accepting defeat in advance rather than running the risk of battle. Now in a world where everything is bound up together, who can decide in advance the limits of our influence, or of the work to which one day we might be called?

And yet there is also much pride in the idea that anything whatsoever depends exclusively on us, even though it is true that our free will dwells in a secret place of the heart where our response is freely made, and can never be forced. On the other hand, the resources at our disposal, the consequences of our actions, the very stimulation of our will itself together with the grace which supports it—all these together infinitely transcend the reach of our will. And the man who is at once the strongest and the happiest is he who is so perfectly attuned to the order of the world that he can no longer distinguish between what is the result of his initiative and what of exterior circumstances.

The Stoics established a wider gulf between the world and ourselves than the facts admit. There is nothing which does not depend on us in some way or other: we are collaborators in the whole work of creation. But there is nothing which depends wholly on us, and the very ability to raise my little finger is a gift that has been given me; my part is solely to accept or to refuse the gift.

It is not when we are most supremely happy that we feel our autonomy most clearly, it is at moments of privation and distress. This is undoubtedly what the Stoics were saying. For what can depend wholly on us if it is not keeping our faith in life when the joy of life is taken from us?

5 Homely virtue

The word "neighbor" as used in the Gospel is full of meaning, as is the idea that the love of one's neighbor is the whole duty of man. Even Nietzsche ironically observes that he who puts society above the individual puts the man who is far away above the one who is close at hand.

In the same sense one may say that all the virtues are those of man in his private capacity, and that the virtue of the public man consists in never acting otherwise than as a private citizen.

Our real life is a humble and commonplace affair, known only to the very small number of people who are bound to us as closely as it is possible to be (for those whose aim is to make a show, or to distinguish themselves on a larger stage, are not interested in such things). It is composed of an infinite number of emotions, thoughts, and actions which, at every moment of time, give us real contact with the things and persons around us. Once outside our narrow circle they all slip through our fingers; what we do, say, and feel becomes less private and personal, the effects cease to depend on us.

We must not despise all those little events which, though fleeting, nevertheless fill the passing hours of each day, all those incidents of our daily life which leave no trace behind and awaken no echo. Our whole being is wholly involved in them; they are the only ones which have a full and lively meaning for us, and which, indeed, enable us at every moment to establish contact with the absolute. If every man could fix his attention upon them and devote himself entirely to them, there would be no further need of the important schemes by which we seek to change the face of the earth. It would be changed without our intervention.

6 *On avoiding quarrels*

We must avoid the intolerable attitude of those who spend their life quarreling with themselves, and with others.

We often strive for victory in a contest whose issue is of little importance to us, and in which our heart is really on our adversary's side: the only thing that matters is that we should win, not that we should be right. We must refrain from every dispute in which the victory counts for more than what one wins by it. If the defeat of our enemy is also the defeat of the truth, it is our defeat too. It follows that the battles over ideas are more to be feared than any other, for they stimulate men's *amour-propre* in the very domain where it is our especial duty to subdue it. Every dispute darkens the inner light: the wise man perceives this light precisely because he preserves his soul in peace. And if he is wrong, he finds more happiness in giving way than he would have found in a triumph; for in the latter case he merely keeps what he already had, in the former he gains something new.

Our relations with another must never take the form of a trial of strength in which one must win and the other lose. Two persons are not in the world as two boxers, one of whom is destined to win, and the other to be beaten. Rather, they are two mediators, seeking a common good; and what either finds is profitable to the other. It has often been said that humanity is like a single man realizing himself through the variety of individuals and the successive generations: the individuals are bound together in a unity just as our mental states are, either constantly, or only at certain moments. Like them, men strive for pre-eminence, and it is not always the best who achieve it. But in our relations with others, as with our relations with ourselves, we should allow a hearing to every individual, and then reconcile them, making them support each other, and work together.

7 *Gentleness in our relations with other men*

Gentleness is the remedy for all evils engendered by *amourpropre* (a certain sort of indifference cures them too, but only by destroying us in the process). Nor is gentleness with oneself the easiest form of this virtue. Many people live in a permanent state of impatience and irritation, not with others but with themselves; and when others become involved it is merely sparks from this fire that burn them.

Gentleness is inseparable from humility. The man who is full of himself writhes under the smallest offense; he is always furious with himself, but at the same time is forever complaining that others lack consideration. On the other hand, the man who never expects anything, and who cannot imagine that he deserves anything, habitually sees in another some good trait which fills him with joy, or perhaps some weakness which awakens his sympathy and which he tries to help.

There is no deep relationship between men that is not founded on gentleness; all the others are merely formal; underneath lie the hostility and contempt, barely disguised, which separate men and make union impossible. Nothing but gentleness enables individual men to recognize their separateness, and at the same time to support each other, enjoying communion in the consciousness of their mutual weakness. The practice of gentleness enables us to treat each other with a consideration at once natural and understanding. This indeed makes all our hurts more painful still by bringing them into the open, but only to relieve them and to heal them. Gentleness is not the same as indulgence for the faults of another; rather it is the recognition of his existence and his presence in the world. With the practice of gentleness, his mere existence ceases to be an offense to us; we no longer try to thwart him or destroy him; we accept him; we are happy that he should be. We enjoy his existence, so to say, with him. We see it as an invitation to a spiritual cohabitation, physical cohabitation being no more than an image of this. Gentleness is active good will towards other men, not for what they are only, but for what they might be. It enables us to see many possibilities which a rougher hand would force underground or blight, and which, perhaps, would never come to the light of day and bear fruit were it not for the attention and confidence we have shown.

Gentleness enables us to accept all the laws of our human condition, and in so doing, to rise superior to them. He who revolts against these laws shows how deeply he resents them and is their slave, but he who accepts them in a spirit of gentleness penetrates through them, and fills them with light. Of these laws also it must be said that their yoke is easy and their burden light.[3]

8 Gentleness and firmness

Of all the virtues, gentleness is both the subtlest and the rarest, especially today; and at all times it is the most difficult to hold fast and to practice. People sometimes confuse it with weakness, flabbiness, or insipidity. When the will intervenes, however slightly, it becomes a sham, and revolts us. True gentleness is so considerate, so tactful, and so active that, when we meet it, we are always astonished that it can do us so much good, while at the same time apparently giving us nothing.

Gentleness is not, as is often thought, the contrary of firmness; it is the sheen on its surface. Firmness should not stay the painter's hand but hold it steady, and often the purity of a delicate contour has the power to cool passion and to direct it aright. The union of gentleness and firmness is sometimes so perfect that they become indistinguishable, both to him who exercises them and to the other man: the former is only conscious of yielding to an irresistible impulse and a natural grace, the latter of hearing another's appeal and feeling another's support.

Gentleness is so far from being the opposite of firmness that it is in fact the only true strength. It dissolves every form of opposition. The strongest man is not he who dominates passion, his or another's, with a violent effort, but he who tames it with the gentleness of reason. The will stiffens when another would bend or break it, but relaxes in the presence of gentleness. Only gentleness wins battles without fighting them, and transforms foes into friends. There is such a thing as false gentleness: it immediately excites a violent reaction; but true gentleness is more powerful than violence; it makes it unnecessary, and melts it away. For gentleness is not a lack of energy, as is commonly believed, but energy leashed and tamed. It is not the will become slack, but the will transcended, and which has ceased to need to brace itself; it imitates Nature but transfigures her, for Nature knows no gentleness, but only inertia on the one hand, and fury on the other.

9 *Gentleness and light*

The life of the mind and the search for truth are impossible for him who is a stranger to gentleness. Animosity, bitterness, sourness are marks of *amour-propre*. They have the tell-tale smell of the flesh, and this infects the best and noblest thoughts of a man.

Some scientists pursue truth as though they were going into battle. They fancy that she gives up her secrets only to those who bring her to bay by the rigor of their demonstrations, or by torturing her with their instruments. But with this kind of violence, although truth may be taken by surprise, she will never become our ally. If the mind is to know her, the thinker must be docile and sensitive enough to follow the subtly sinuous contours of reality. Truth requires him to achieve a sort of co-operation with the real, a sort of coincidence even, the perfection of which will be, in fact, exactly proportionate to his gentleness. We must listen to truth's answers to our questions, holding ourselves in a sort of immobility and inner silence. She demands of us a pliant attention, one which foreshadows acceptance, together with respect and love. The moment one tries to force her or to take her by storm, she becomes refractory, and shrinks away.

We must silence the tumult of the passions, master the blind reactions of instinct, and attain to the perfection of inward gentleness, before reality will look on us open-eyed, as a friend. Every event, circumstance, and person met with on our way can be reacted to either violently, or with gentleness. Many prefer violence; they love turmoil, excitement. A certain number, either by nature or by choice, opt for insensibility, which they call wisdom. Only a few know the heaven-born spirit of gentleness, which penetrates with light the air we breathe, and spiritualizes everything it touches.

Gentleness is daughter of the light. Our first reactions spring always from a natural impulse, but when Nature is tamed and softened by light, she dissolves into gentleness. And gentleness is at the opposite end of the scale to indifference, for this light, from the moment of its birth, radiates with love. Gentleness is therefore not the opposite of fervor, but rather the most perfect and purified expression of it. And if Pyrrho, the prince of skeptics, practiced true gentleness as is reported of him, there must have been, behind all his intellectual doubts, a subtly sensitive participation with being and life, which many of his contemporaries who confidently dogmatized on the same problems might have envied.

10 *Patience and gentleness*

Patience is bearing what must be borne, and then waiting; it is harder than acting and deciding. It is the virtue of life in time. If such a life is to be bearable we cannot do without patience. In the first place we must have the secret of filling time when it appears to be empty; and there can be no better way than patience, which is a sort of gentleness in our relations with time, to which we refuse to do violence, nor wish to abolish.

But, contrary to the general view, patience involves more than waiting; it implies endurance, and endurance implies both pain felt and pain accepted. Can it be said that being the virtue most closely connected with time and suffering, patience cannot be other than a sort of resignation, and that therefore it cannot be creative, and is inevitably joyless? There is, it is true, a negative form of patience, that of the man who is incapable of anything more than bearing life's trials; and bearing life itself as a trial. But there is also the positive form; here suffering is not only accepted, but willed. Patience greets suffering, when it comes, without recrimination, she accepts it without complaint. She does not take pride in her misfortunes as if hers were an exceptional destiny, and she one of the elect. She does not seek to revenge herself on all who are spared. She takes it as a gift which she must love and make her own, a part of herself and her life.

This form of patience keeps the soul active, and even joyful, in the midst of adversity. She bears every frustration without yielding to anger, or to any of the impulses rooted in self-love. She converts the first flush of impatience into gentleness.

In the deepest recess of her heart, she holds the secret of pursuing a course of action whose result she cannot foresee, and perhaps will never see. In that case she is justly known as perseverance. Neither the intoxication of prosperity nor that of misfortune can blind her.

Patience is a stranger to indifference: she never gives up the struggle. Patience demands much courage, and much faith. She must stay my hand from acting; she never anticipates the right moment to act. She does not lose heart, even when time fails to keep the promises of eternity; for she is not waiting in the expectation of eternity; she is there already. To have before one time which cures all ills is to know that nothing in time is ever finished and complete, and this is already to have penetrated beyond all time.

Patience is perhaps the supreme virtue of the will. "To be impatient," says Fénelon,[4] "is to desire what one has not, and not to want what one has." When we will the ill that afflicts us, it is not an ill; why make it an ill by refusing to will it?

11 *A presence which passes our understanding*

Habit makes me blind and dulls my mind to all the extraordinary things of which the world is full—light, movement, my own existence, you who are speaking to me and who, suddenly, come towards me with friendship in your eyes; and yet, were there no such thing as habit, I would be surrounded exclusively by objects of terror and miraculous presences. The child is well aware that when he fixes his eyes for a moment on the things he knows best, and suddenly forgets their habitual use, they are the ones which leave him thunderstruck. And the most perfect art is that which shows us afresh the things we know best, as if, in a new revelation, we were seeing them for the first time. So it is that were it not for the force of habit, reality would strike our senses so directly and so violently that we could not bear its impact. Habit is a sort of protective shield.

Now spiritual activity in all its forms is an attempt not to acquire habits, as some say, but to break them, so as to uncover the fabulous spectacle beneath—which habit hides, and always distorts. And so men do very wrong to scorn the humble object beneath their eyes, to dream sterile dreams of the future, to imagine on the other side of the grave a world which will finally realize their desires. The whole of reality is already given to them; the difficulty is to obtain an undistorted image of it. It is not by going beyond appearances, as is commonly said, that we will ultimately grasp the truth, for our need precisely is that truth should appear to us, and the greatest minds reveal what before had escaped us, and what habit will cover over again soon enough. Neither behind phenomena, nor beyond the grave, does there exist a reality other than the one we see today; some reject it and chase after fantasies, while others find in it, according to the measure of their love, all the joys of earth, together with the joys of Paradise.

Notes

1. See Ch. XII, sections 6 and 7, *et. seq.*

2. French philosopher, 1782–1854.

3. cf. Matt. 11:30.

4. Bishop of Cambrai; one of the most brilliant minds of the reign of Louis XIV (1651–1715).

CHAPTER XI

THE DOUBLE nature of man, physical and spiritual, is the source of his special character, his liberty, his power of choice; therefore each side of his nature must be preserved. The attempt to suppress either is futile and harmful, for, like the self-regulating order of the world, the soul has its own compensatory and self-regulating mechanism.[1] Wisdom is this balance attained; reason is her instrument.

Passion is that which sees in its object an absolute good: we have an experience of the absolute when we experience passion. But we must realize that the objects of human passion can only be images of the absolute rather than the absolute itself. Perhaps the only true object of passion is the inner vision which we undertake to incarnate.

If wisdom is nature and spirit held in balance, heroism is nature tamed and subjugated, and holiness nature transfigured.

Wisdom and the Passions

※

1 *Our dual nature*

The deeper the roots of a tree descend into the darkness of
the earth, the higher will rise the leafy branches, delicately rus-
tling in the realms of light. And the majestic immobility of the
tree is in reality an equilibrium of ceaseless movement, in which
all the forces of nature are active and correlated, counter-balanc-
ing and counter-checking one another with a precision more
wonderful than any form of anarchic liberty.

Each of us resembles the tree. The most obscure, the deepest,
and frequently the basest and most selfish passions lie buried in
the depths of his heart; it is these which often constitute its principal nourishment. The purest love is always miraculously
bound up with them. If this were not so, the love would soon
cease to be our own; and instead of rising boldly, like the tree's
fragile shoots, into the impalpable blue of the sky, it would
gradually dissipate into nothing.

Nature and mythology are full of parables expressing this
truth. The butterfly is a grub—with wings; and the man who
flies highest in the world of the spirit is he who carries his grub
with him to heaven. The centaur, the sphinx, and the siren express the idea that man emerges out of an animal, and that he
never sheds his hoofs, his claws, his scales. Man is a mixture; his
dual nature is what makes him man; it is the essence of his vocation and destiny. It is folly to imagine him a god or to reduce
him to an animal; he is more like a satyr with two natures, and it

would be hard to say whether his deepest desire is to raise the animal within him to the contemplation of the divine light, or to bring the god down into his animal body, and make him feel every impulse coursing through his flesh.

Man's reason is itself a balance held between two instincts, one animal, which imprisons him within himself, the other spiritual which makes him forget his prison. Reason is the link between the body and the spirit and keeps the balance between them, the body restraining the spirit from soaring too high, the spirit preventing the body from sinking too low. Without this double nature, how could we choose what we would be? Our freedom springs from it. And if reason never succeeds entirely in identifying either with the angel or the animal within us, it is nevertheless that which gives the victory now to one, now to the other.

Within each one of us a kind of vertical oscillation takes place, operating in the very center of his being. This alternating rise and fall constitutes the very life of his consciousness. With the same resources, some raise themselves up to Heaven, others fall down to Hell.

2 *Joining the extremes*

Temperateness[2] is neither mediocrity nor weakness. It is rather a sort of inner plenitude. To temper oneself is to conform one's self to the universe, and this is what enables a man to be himself, and master of himself. This in turn involves holding together the two extremes within him, rather than ignoring them, or else yielding to them. For temperateness needs them both; the temperate man bears them along, so to say, within himself; he must not refuse to acknowledge, or attempt to suppress, either of them. So far from being a central point, equidistant from each, temperateness fills the whole space between them and thus unites them. It modifies each of the principles— not, however, by diminishing its intensity, but by the strength with which it cleaves to the other at the same time. It will not be shifted from the central position, for here alone vision can reach far enough and feeling deep enough for the union and reconciliation of the opposites to become possible, without the self being torn in two. The truly temperate man can contemplate the infinities of being with a steady eye.

Temperateness is both tension and understanding. Its result is that each thing has its proper place, while each faculty functions most naturally and most efficaciously, supported by the functioning of the others; each is regulated by the others, and profits from their exercise. It is the union of all the potentialities of the self, in co-operation with all the potentialities of the universe, the self finding in the latter both its limits and a support. Desire is, by its very nature, infinite and insatiable, which means that we never quite reach or take possession of anything at all. And wisdom does not consist, as is often believed, in renouncing the absolute; on the contrary it is a meeting with the absolute[3] which gives each thing its "measure."

In mathematics, all problems are problems of proportion and limits; it is not otherwise in human life. Each one of our acts expresses a relationship between us and the universe, a relationship which defines our true measure. All these acts themselves tend and reach out towards a limit; this is our essence; and of the essence one can say both that it transcends our acts and is their foundation.

3 Compensation

Because I am dual, a being whose essence is realized by the maintenance of an equilibrium between two extremes, neither what is noblest in me, nor what is basest, quite seems to be me. We have within us the gift of consciousness, which is at one and the same time vision, command, and aspiration; this is the divine part of ourselves. But we also have a being which is the object of this vision, which rebels against the command, and is unfaithful to the aspiration; this is the part of ourselves which belongs to Nature. The self is the connecting link between the divine and the animal parts; in it, the spirit takes flesh and the flesh is spiritualized.

Temperateness is an act; its perfection is proportionate to the resistance it has to overcome, and to the effort this entails. The greatest art requires the most resistant medium, but triumphs over it—and the most powerful inspiration, but the artist holds it in check. In the noblest activity, and even in the purest love, one can always find anger which has been dominated.

For every excess is a sign of weakness and not of strength, and no excess fails to receive its punishment in the final count. The thirst for knowledge can be an excess, and is so when it becomes an ambition of the intellect, developing into a sort of covetousness, or else a mere pastime, despising action and deterring a man from it, instead of being the foundation of action and its light. And it is even possible to have an excess of virtue. In this case, it is difficult to decide whether the soul is tempting nature or tempting God; but it is certainly a sign of lack of humility, a confidence in oneself and in one's own resources which destroys the sense of one's limitations, blinding us to the true relationship between our nature and our will. An excess of virtue will force events one day to give it the lie and bring it to nothing.

Every time one fails to realize temperateness, a compensating reaction takes place, and equilibrium is restored. Instinct asserts itself at another spot, unobserved, and with the same intensity as it sought the original outlet which the will had blocked. And when held in check, it paralyzes by its inertia the will which checked it. Inversely, should one try to sacrifice thought to action, the power of reflection would be born again, but only to waste itself in dreams; or else it would introduce an extravagant or wayward element into action from which one hoped to exclude it altogether.

4 *On the threshold of consciousness*

Is it true that quite close to us, just beyond the threshold of consciousness, there exists a terrifying and fantastic world which is in fact ourselves, even though we do not suspect its presence? But how can it really belong to us, so long as we are not aware of it, and have no control over it? You may reply that this fantastic world suddenly explodes into our consciousness, taking us each time by surprise, but causing a commotion in us such as makes it impossible to deny that it is part of ourselves. What then is this fatality which takes shape within me, while I stand by, a helpless spectator? I can only say "me" when my mind begins to understand, and my will begins to identify with these obscure impulsions, or alternatively to repudiate them. This dark, violent world may be as close to me as it is possible to be, it is not me. Does it even exist in its own right until my consciousness gives it life, either to subdue it and to still its clamor, or else to give it rein and to stimulate it further? There is nothing in ourselves which properly deserves to be called the unconscious, nothing but consciousness forever coming to be, alive to all allurements without, to all the solicitations of the flesh and of the senses, to the many voices of public opinion and to all the promptings of passion, a consciousness which is continually extending, deepening, and purifying—or degenerating, according to the reception it accords them.

Without consciousness I would be nothing, not even a thing. This is what gives me being, enabling me at the same time to realize that it is *my* being. It stands between Nature, which transcends it but remains below, and reason, which transcends it too, but from above. Both are at its disposal, and that is why one may say that it is at once the best and the worst of all things. Sometimes it becomes the slave of Nature, even using all the sophistries of reason to pervert and to defile her. Or else, by subordinating Nature to reason, it spiritualizes and transfigures her.

5 Ecstasy

The soul is like a fire which has been put in our keeping, and which it is for us to tend; it is our duty to provide it with nothing but the purest matter. It is not enough to say that, like fire, it purifies everything it touches, for the quality of the flame depends on what feeds it. It may produce a dark smoke which reduces its light, and even its heat, to nothing; it may go out, leaving nothing in the hearth but bitter ashes or burnt-out charcoal.

There are various sorts of ecstasy belonging to each of the faculties of the soul, from the noblest to the lowest. The special function of the reason is to discriminate between them, not to abolish them. Shall it be said that the simplest and the strongest natures are those who experience all the impalpable touches of the psychic life without ever being intoxicated by any? Or should we only say that they know one form of ecstasy only— that of pure water, or reconquered innocence; and that they find new inspiration in the presence of every event, abolishing, as innocence does, all inner division, every shred of *amour-propre*, every excess of the imagination, every shadow of self-indulgence or of perversity?

6 Reason, the faculty which appraises

Reason is the noblest of all our faculties, provided that we do not use it for argumentation but for *appraisal*. Rather than exhausting its strength and ingenuity in extracting subtle deductions from some supposed truth, as yet not proved by experience, it must remain the power which weighs all things, which means that it gives each thing its proper place and its value within the All, while remaining ever mindful of the presence of the All.

The rule of reason does not consist in suppressing the passions, as is often thought, but in a discipline imposed upon them; and this is to confirm them, to give them light, and efficacity. To appeal to reason first of all is to say "no" to life before life begins. He is not reasonable who is inert and without feeling, either by nature or through the use of his reason, but rather he who, possessing the most intense life and the strongest passions, draws from them the impetus to rise, matter to be shaped, and the expansive energy in which he will manifest and express himself.

Reason herself has a certain poetry of her own, a sort of abstract ecstasy. And that is why, though rationality is the badge of mediocrity to those who put their whole faith in inspiration, she may well be folly and delusion to those who trust only what they touch and see.

Just as the crater of an extinct volcano fills with pure water, so the fires of the most violent passions leave behind a sort of pool which they have carved out of the soul; this gradually becomes transparent and reflects the whole sky.

7 Passion and the absolute

We must not despise passion. It reveals the meaning of our destiny, it excites, exalts, and unifies all the potentialities of our being, and brings the absolute and the infinite into every event of our life. Those who despise it are those who are incapable of feeling it. Prudent natures find it alarming, timid hearts bewildering. But passion needs to be stimulated far more often than checked.

Some men remain forever spectators on the side-line, forever holding back and refusing to join the game. Passion never comes their way; and when they see it in others, they condemn it, though not without a touch of jealousy. They will contend that passion makes men reckless, and biased. But the truth is that they lack the strength of character and generosity of spirit to bring to passion. All they see is its most exterior effects, when we are submerged by it and apparently overcome; they see the convulsions of the first moments, or the moment when it is threatened by some obstacle—in a word, before we have mastered it.

Passion is the contrary of emotion. Emotion is indissolubly attached to an event, and it carries us no further than ourselves. Passion begins in us, and transforms the event. Emotion is expectation; it draws its strength from time; but passion is a presence, it draws its strength from eternity; time is not its master, it has become its servant. Emotion demands of time a moment at which it will return to tranquility, whereas passion needs no such limit, it needs infinity to subsist. It asks of time nothing but occasions to express itself. It is pure receptivity and consent to the inner impulsion, and total imperviousness to any voice coming from without which would seduce it out of its course.

If the object of passion has infinite value, it follows that this object is what the philosophers call "an end in itself." And so it cannot be either a thing, as the miser or the man of ambition thinks, or an individual, as the lover imagines, or an ideal, which is how the hero conceives it; on the contrary, it must be a living absolute, for which these are substituted, and which provide us with a sort of image of it. And it is important that we should realize that they are, in fact, but images.

Consequently, passion cannot do without the co-operation of free will and of reason; but it must have them as allies, and not as slaves. Animals do not feel passion.

8 *Passions good and bad*

Everyone will agree that passion can be sometimes good, and bad at other times. We now have a fairly satisfactory criterion of its value. It may originate in itself, or outside itself. In the first instance, the self is seeking to extend itself, and with this in mind aims at an exterior object which is really finite, but which it takes to be infinite. In the second, the man's aim is to go deeper into himself by discovering in the depths of his finite essence an infinite destination. And the result is that the first man will never find a resting-place, since he applies an infinite aspiration to a finite object which disappoints him as soon as he attains it, while the second finds his rest in the infinite aspiration itself, and this never disappoints him, since no finite object hems it in or arrests its flight. When passion finds a resting-place within itself, this is sufficient proof that our life has discovered, in this passion, its true goal, and that the absolute has become present to us, enlightening us, and supporting and nourishing us. For the absoluteness of passion can only be explained by the hypothesis that a man has met the absolute *in* his passion. And this is sufficient to make clear how the movement of the soul, at once tending to the absolute and proceeding from it, can be at one and the same time active and passive, which is precisely the character of every genuine passion.

Passion is bad when it causes confusion in the body and the soul, and when the meddling intelligence sits in judgement upon it, the confusion is only aggravated. It is good when it invigorates body and mind, and brings them together in harmony.

An evil passion fills the heart with darkness and distress, a good one brings peace to the heart, and light.

An evil passion questions the value of its object and its relation to us, a good one is concerned with the second point only.

An evil passion always seeks to justify itself by argument, though it never quite succeeds; for the arguments are sophistries. A good passion has no need of such, it scorns them: a glimpse of the object is enough to reassure us. The first enslaves us to ourselves, or rather to our bodies, the other delivers us from this bondage, and so sets free the soul. The former destroys the meaning of life, the latter gives it its meaning. The former demolishes, and the latter creates our self and the world.

9 *The virtue of passion*

One is constantly told that passion is a madness, that it enslaves us, disorganizes our lives and destroys our freedom. And yet we are all searching for a passion of another kind, one that surmounts the opposition of instinct and will, creating a perfect unity in the mind; one that gathers all the powers of the soul around a single point and sets it free, rather than holding it prisoner. The word itself admirably expresses its double nature, since it designates the most intense activity we are capable of, and yet it is wholly given; totally spontaneous, it demands no effort, effort never being necessary except to restrain it. In it are joined movement and repose, both in their perfect state: perfect movement, since it is tending to an infinite and inexhaustible object, and perfect repose, since in the very movement which is of its nature, the man is enabled both to discover himself and to fulfill himself.

Every man is searching for a passion worthy of filling his soul to capacity. So long as he has failed to find it, his existence is lifeless, joyless, deprived of light and of any goal worthy of the name; it is a problem to which he has not yet found the key. He is lost in a world which has shown him no value to which he can dedicate himself, in other words, sacrifice himself. True passion is essentially selfless and generous; we are not trying to acquire anything, we want to remake the world.

So far from rending our soul and abandoning it to distress and impotence, it brings us inner certitude, equilibrium, tranquility and peace. It puts an end to all convulsions in the soul: it gives them no time to appear. It marks the end of doubt, hesitation, and inertia. We do not question it, for through it we have found our way and our salvation; all our concern is for the object of our passion, since we can never be sure we are giving it the attention it deserves. Nothing else enables a man to become conscious of the power by which he realizes himself, and to know that his destiny and his vocation are one and the same.

No one brings with him at birth a passion ready formed. It must appear at the end of a long period of waiting, at the moment when life reaches its summit. We tremble as we begin to feel its approach. It is the sign that we have left behind us the period of trials and experiments, that our life is totally committed, all inner divisions abolished; nor will we ever again have to make a fresh start. Perhaps it might be said that there is no passion in our soul other than the pure idea for which we are responsible, and which we undertake to incarnate.[4]

10 Wisdom, which is self-possession

Wisdom is at one and the same time a property of the intelligence and of the will. We can justifiably call her a property of the will, since she imposes order on our desires and passions. But she is the property of intelligence too, because she discerns the order to be imposed. She is the cure for a double error: firstly, that idea that we can only find happiness in the continuous expansion of our being until it coincides with the All; and secondly that we must forever turn our eyes away from what we have and reach out after what we have not, for this leaves us equally dissatisfied whether we attain it or not.

Wisdom is the discovery and the love of our essence, of the being which has been given us, and the universe which spreads out before our eyes; of the situation in which we find ourselves and its attendant obligations. It is the death of envy, for it is the realization that the inner life[5] of the world into which every man penetrates the moment he says "I" is so precious a thing that nothing else could possibly be worth more, or be more highly desired. From now onwards, nothing counts but the use to which he puts this discovery; and this is precisely what has been entrusted to him.

It is clear how wrong it is to think of wisdom as a negative attitude and a renunciation of great things which always includes a touch of prosiness and insensibility. It is the reverse of these; it is the courage which is demanded if we are to attribute an incomparable value to the humblest things, once we become aware that they have been entrusted to us as the instruments with which to work out our destiny.

Wisdom is the ability to possess oneself rather than to dominate oneself. It transforms the parcel of being which is given to us into a good, ever present, and indefinitely increasing. We slowly acquire a subtle and powerful art; we do not devalue the finite by comparison with the infinite, but rather we learn to find the infinite in the finite. So far from separating me from the world, I discover ever new relationships between the world and myself, responses coming from the world to appeals coming from me, and appeals coming from the world to which I must respond.

The wise man can always be recognized by an extremely delicate sensitivity, with the consequence that the world contains no object which fails to awaken an echo in his heart, teaching him something or requiring something of him. At the opposite end of the scale, the blind of heart remains ever alone, and the fool always acts too soon or too late.

11 *Wisdom, heroism, and holiness*

Wisdom is effortlessness acquired by effort, a return to spontaneous and authentic activity; she is nourished by the light which enlightens her; her garment is pleasure; it is her grace, not her preoccupation; she radiates good will.

One may truly say that she is at once Nature in equilibrium and Nature idealized. She appears to be rest rather than movement, but this is because she does not yield to any particular passion or momentary impulse, but dominates each one. Inevitably one associates her with moderation, which is the secret of her rule, and with experience, which has taught her what she knows. There is a false wisdom which is nothing more than a lack of vitality; it is seen in the over-obedient child, and in the old man in whom the life-force has begun to fail. True wisdom is always violent feeling held in rein. The common belief is that wisdom consists in passive acceptance of what one has and in the mortification of desire. The truth is that she has transferred the infiniteness of desire from what she lacks to what she possesses; that because she asks for nothing, she constantly receives everything; that with the minimum of matter she creates a work of art whose nature is purely spiritual.

Heroism, unlike wisdom, is a virtue which cannot easily be preserved without respite throughout a lifetime; when it appears to be continuous, the fact is that it is coming to a new birth at every instant. Unlike wisdom, it is not a harmonization of nature and spirit, nor of the temporal and the eternal. It is a victory of the spirit over rebellious nature, a violent eruption of eternity into time. The satisfaction it brings is the contrary of pleasure, whose allurements the hero always resists. One always associates heroism with the ideas of suffering deliberately inflicted on the body, of self-sacrifice and of death.

Holiness is a tranquil certitude, a passion at peace, which sets a man in a world above that of nature, but by which the world of nature is illuminated. It is often thought that holiness is a victory over nature, but this is not so. Here nature is not humiliated or annihilated, as she is in the case of heroism, or disciplined or subjugated, as she is by wisdom; she is transfigured. Nature yields voluntarily to holiness and becomes her ally and companion. She renounces her appetites, but her energies are incalculably increased. We may say that she rises above herself. She seems to have been abrogated, but the truth is that she has become the living body of holiness. Holiness seems to be a new nature; she is, in fact, at once nature renounced and nature fulfilled.[6]

Notes

1. cf. Ch. IV, section 4.

2. Fr. *la mesure*. The word "temperateness" suggests *restraint*, but *tempérer* originally meant "to mix," "to blend."

3. This idea will be explained and developed in sections 7–9 of this chapter.

4. Ten years later, Lavelle wrote: "If a person who is not free is nothing but a thing, it is understandable that liberty is the only good which we can desire absolutely. In reality it is beyond all goods, since without it there is no good which we can call ours, and which it is possible for us to enjoy." *Les Puissances du Moi*, p. 143.

5. Fr. *intimité*.

6. In the last year of his life, Lavelle returned to the theme of the final section of this chapter. In *Quatre Saints*, the last volume he was to publish before his death in the same year, there is a comparison between the spirit of wisdom, heroism, and holiness, on the same lines as here, but treated in greater detail.

CHAPTER XII

THE OBJECT of all knowledge is an appearance; and this is precisely what we need, a reality that *appears*, that is *revealed*. Nevertheless, we cannot remain permanently content with this; we must try to penetrate to reality itself. Since knowledge fails to give it to us, we must try another way. The only other way is participation. For being, while transcending knowledge, includes it.

What, then, is implied in participation? It is living in a state of detachment (either permanently, like the saint, or at intervals, like the rest of us) from all mere appearances, whether these be material things, or hopes, desires, fears, and regrets.

The first result of even an effort to accomplish this is the beginning of communion with others; the second, the beginning of knowledge, but a knowledge that goes beyond appearances, to the meaning of things.

This state of consciousness Lavelle calls "purity." In the final section of the chapter he gives a description of it, and of the powers which it releases. This is not the beatific vision, in which the manifested world, totally transcended, is finally blotted out; it is rather the first step which the soul takes in the ascent to this vision.

Spiritual Space

❧

1 *The properties of knowledge*

Knowledge is the characteristic property of man; it makes him divine. It brings him into touch with what transcends him. It detaches him from himself, and thereby continually enriches him. It raises him from the life of the moment, that of the body, to eternal life, which is the life of ideas.[1]

But a certain avidity with which *amour-propre* pursues knowledge makes her face shine with a dazzling light; this is a reflection of man's covetousness rather than a property of the light itself. Knowledge, which brings us into the presence of the All, should abolish self-love rather than serve it; disinterestedness is her very essence. And yet knowledge does in fact enlarge to its own measure the knowing self, while at the same time detaching it from itself ever more completely. There is a correspondence between the mind which knows and the knowledge it acquires, but though one may say that the quality of the mind determines that of the knowledge it can attain, the converse is also true.

We possess nothing except what knowledge brings us, for knowledge is the wholly interior and personal possession of what is beyond me, which however the self contrives to embrace and contain. It is equally true to say that the knowing mind goes out from itself to be present to the world, and that it enters into itself, bringing the world with it. Knowledge is indeed a sort of frontier between the self and the world, but one which makes possible every sort of communication exchange between them. At first it is a mere spectacle to which we treat ourselves; but this spectacle is soon traversed and shot through by countless tracks which our will and desires leave in their wake. It is the term and goal of all our activity; and even when it seems to be nothing more than a means of further activity, the truth is that the goal of this latter is itself to extend knowledge further. Man always rebels against a law imposed on him from without; instinctively he doubts its validity, and suspects that somebody's interest is present in disguise. He seeks to act in the full light of knowledge, and desires that knowledge should be sufficient to motivate his acts.

But what can we know? It would be illogical to assert that the object of knowledge could be the faculty which knows—that faculty which can only come into play in the knowledge of something other than itself. All knowledge is, therefore, knowledge of some object or other, and, as such, it cannot satisfy us: it is an image, which merely tickles our curiosity. But the object can acquire significance if it becomes the means of mediation between me and you—if, with its help, we have access to a world where we cease to be alone. Here, an encounter with a self which is not mine illuminates my own self, together with a spiritual world of which we may say both that it transcends us, and that it belongs to each of us. When this occurs, knowledge, which is always relative, has become a road leading to a revelation which is absolute.

2 *From the without to the within*

Only knowledge is capable of encompassing all that is, as knowledge in principle can do; it is only of knowledge that one can say that it encompasses everything as light does, for light, like knowledge, does not pick and choose between the objects it illuminates. The destination of knowledge is thus universal, and that being so, we should not demand of man that he should come to know himself, but rather the world; here, so far from being one object among others, he is nothing but the act of knowing, the object of which is the world, and not himself. But all knowledge should go from the without to the within, though for most men, it stops at the object, in other words, at the without. Thus for the scientist there is no within; reality is for him nothing more than a perceived appearance. He goes no further than the manifested form of things; his whole aim is to eliminate the inner initiative which makes them to be, so that he may calculate the principles in accordance with which they act upon each other; for these are what he can grasp, and subsequently make use of. Beyond all these mutual relationships, which are constant, though the events themselves are never the same, there is that which the delicate meshes of the net of scientific inquiry cannot capture and hold fast, namely, reality itself—reality which meets me at the present moment, in its uniqueness, and in a form which is itself unique and unrepeatable. Reality eludes science, which closes in on it from every side, but never succeeds in laying hold of it.

When it is a question of the knowledge of human beings, and not of things, the situation is entirely different. The without is here nothing but a sign. Acts and faces are but symbols; their sole interest is what they signify. Scientific laws help me not at all to know the individual now before me. I focus my attention upon him; I know he must obey these laws, but I do not know how he differs from other individuals who must obey them too. However what I am looking for as I watch him is not the external things which influence him and which he cannot change, for these express what he is not, rather than what he is; I am looking for the freedom which he exercises, sometimes without knowing it, for were it not for this I would relegate him to the domain of things, and would cease to *consider* him, in both senses of the word.

The rule which we apply to our knowledge of other people,

namely never to stop at words or acts, but to penetrate to meanings and intentions, clearly shows where, in every domain, we
must seek the truly real. In all things, as here, it resides in their
inwardness[2] and their spirituality, of which we see nothing but
the appearance—an appearance which often distorts the truth,
but which is nearly always as far as we go.

3 *Spiritual space*

Men differ from one another in the extent and the purity of
the spiritual space which they succeed in creating around themselves. Each of us is imprisoned in a wall of matter, which turns
him into a slave and a solitary. But his desires constantly push
his horizon back, and his intelligence pierces it in all directions.
Thus a luminous atmosphere spreads out further and further
around us, in which each of us can see himself; it liberates his
faculties, enabling them to function easily and freely. It enables
him, further, to discover other things being similar to himself,
encircled by this same wide, luminous horizon, within which
we must first cohabit, but in which, later, we will be able to communicate, according to the measure of the disinterestedness of
our thought and our love.

It is a serious mistake to think that the world of bodies is
common to all, while the world of spirit is private and individual. For in the first place, the world of bodies is public only
because it is a spectacle readily apprehended by our *minds*; our
physical being, on the other hand, is eternally isolated from the
physical being of everyone else, and is continually shot through
by impulsions which are ours and ours alone, impulsions which
we cannot wholly dominate, and which we cannot wholly communicate, nor completely hide, or perfectly know, nor can we
remain entirely unconscious of them. On the other hand,
thought, which is invisible, is a stranger to the limitations of the
body, and will not be imprisoned within them. The marvel is
that it should be in the intimacy of thought that all individuals

can commune together, and acquire a knowledge of physical bodies also which is true for them all.

The only solitaries are those who live alone with their bodies; the dialogue of a man with his body creates a solitude within him, filled with self-love, in which he is without a single companion. But the mind is never alone. It is a pure emptiness, but an emptiness capable of admitting the universe within itself. Obstacles go down before it; nagging preoccupations dissolve away; an infinity of paths opens out before our feet, an infinity of voices assails our ears which from the very first are answers to our own calling.

All men are called to leave material space, the home of constraint, suffering, and warfare, and gradually to learn to live in a spiritual space where reign liberty, peace, and love, and where everything is airy, mobile, and transparent. The eyes light upon objects without being distracted by them. Peacefully and effortlessly the lungs fill with air which seems to come from the depths of being itself. Objects do not resist the hand which stretches out to grasp them; and their contact is firm, gentle, unresisting. Our active powers have broken their chains, and a limitless field opens out before them, and becomes their habitual resting-place. We cannot distinguish now between being acted upon and acting, between what we desire and what we possess, between the reality of the external world and the creations of our will, between our mental states and the shape of things themselves.

As movement enables our body to occupy any point in material space, and to take the place of other bodies, sympathy enables our soul to occupy any point in spiritual space, and to put ourselves in the place of other souls.

In spiritual space, all the barriers thrown up by a man's preoccupations and desires are broken down. His eyes travel round a limitless horizon, and whatever path he follows, he meets nothing but stable and luminous objects, which he can abandon without distress, and meet again without a sense of futility.

4 *The two lights*

In the world, it will be said, there is nothing wholly beautiful, noble, or pure but light. Everything it falls upon or merely touches becomes beautiful, and is ennobled and purified. And though it brings into view the horrors of the world, it takes no stain from them.

And yet it is the shadows cast by light that make us aware of light, and often it is in shadow that we seek its blessings, partly because it shields us from its glare—and yet we see it nigh—partly because in the shadow itself there is light diffused. It is the light of day which makes the beauty of night: night hides in her womb all the mystery of Nature which the coming day will reveal. In night there is both the memory and the promise of day, together with the obscure glow which subsists between twilight and dawn. Night, and the sense of her deep and secret life whose forms and colors gradually come into view with the dawning of day, fill our hearts with indefinable joy. Our feelings themselves are a night, out of which the light of thought ceaselessly emerges. But who would think of separating thought and feeling?

Now there are two kinds of light, one of which is, as it were, but the shadow of the other, though most often we remain satisfied with it. For objects have only to appear before our eyes bathed in the light of the sun for us to forget another light, which lights them from within—a light which we perceive when we close our eyes, and which we must discover by passing through the other, if it is continually to reveal to our understanding souls within bodies.

And if the outer light reveals the relationship of things to our body, the inner light reveals their relationship to our soul, that is to say it reveals the soul of things themselves, what they are, and not merely what they appear to be. This light is love. In love the meaning of life is discovered, the tasks which are given to us cease to be a burden, and the solutions appear before the problems. When it shines in our hearts, we are less aware of the objects which it illuminates than the joy it brings.

5 *The simplicity of spiritual sight*
"If your eye is simple your whole body will be full of light."[3] Simplicity is the condition of any real communication with another man. Nothing else can endow both intelligence and feeling with the perfect delicacy which alone frees the eye of the soul from the film of covetousness, and thus renders seeing clear.

Truth cannot enter a consciousness which is not worthy of her. This is true even of the knowledge of material things, but for these some capacity for attention is all we need. When spiritual truth is the quest, a certain purity of intention is necessary as well, which explains the multitude of blind persons in this domain. And it may be asserted both that the man who rises highest will find the clearest and the purest light, and also that he who most completely clears his soul of all the stains of self-love makes most room to receive it.

Some of the philosophers with the greatest reputations were like industrious mechanics combining their highly polished concepts into ingenious systems. Herein lies a temptation which neither Aristotle, nor Spinoza, nor Hegel altogether resisted. But in quite simple souls one sometimes observes a straight and natural growth which is enough to set them above this impressive greatness.

There is a certain simplicity to be found in the spiritual insight of some simple folk which dissolves all the subtleties and all the insoluble paradoxes of reason, and goes beyond them. With them a multitude of separate little channels become pathways of light, spreading out and converging on the same central point whence it proceeds.

6 Purity

There is a purity in some eyes which expresses the whole person, without any movement on his part, any act, any sign, or any word. These would destroy his unity, and would substitute a passing mental state or volition for his eternal essence. Without projecting any image, and without anything specific in mind, he makes us aware of the reciprocal and unmotivated communication which can exist between different souls who participate in one life, and in the contemplation of the same universe.

The purity of a smile in which all the features are relaxed, has not only ceased to express certain particular emotions and passions; on the contrary, it bears witness to the fact that these have been abolished. Nothing remains but an open-hearted welcome to life, a motionless movement, in which body and spirit have become one. The individual has dissolved away and can be seen no more. What we see is a revelation of a spiritual order whose instrument and vehicle he is.

Purity bears witness to the natural development of a soul rooted in reality, which is fulfilling therein the function that has fallen to its lot with a tranquil ease from which every trace of deception, as of negligence, is absent. The pure in heart reconcile spontaneity and reflection: for reflection being no longer necessary, everything in them now appears to take place spontaneously; and yet this is quite unlike the mechanical reactions of instinct, but resembles rather that act, devoid of movement, by which the soul is present to itself, the act by which its essence is realized.

Purity gives material things a spiritual face. It is a stranger both to premeditation and to effort; it takes no account of merit. It reconciles necessity and liberty, grace and nature. Its companion is a serene joy, born of calm and willing acquiescence in a soul which has already measured the heights and depths of existence, and has accepted in advance any suffering it may bring.

7 *Purification*

Purity is an act of presence to oneself and to the world. No act is more difficult to perform, for every distraction which breaks the unity of our being is impure. Distraction is the soul's propensity for what is foreign to her nature, for what is perishable; it is the first step of a descent into nothingness—we never wholly consent to it. For no one gives himself over to distractions with an undivided will or with total sincerity. Love does not lead us on this path, but lack of love.

Purity creates a void in the soul, but an active void. It combines passive waiting and active attention, self-reliance and friendliness. Purity always leaves our hands free.

Impurity clouds the simplicity of the relationship which ought to exist between the will and our pure essence. It makes us yield to the seduction of objects exterior to us and beneath us; these dislocate and darken the activity of the spirit. To keep one's purity is to be able to hold back; it means holding in passiveness the pure essence of our self, which is God's will in us and for us, refusing to let it be changed from its true nature, for this is the beginning of every sort of corruption.

One can speak of "pure Nature" and also "pure spirit," but there is always the possibility that the will which links them should render both impure.

Purity is the virtue of innocence; we are constantly losing it and finding it again, which is why our spiritual life is nothing but one long work of purification. It is possible to conceive of it in two ways, different but convergent: a negative form, which consists of turning away our eyes from everything, within us and without, which is low and unworthy; but this suffices to produce the positive form, namely, the restoration of what is best in ourselves—spiritual aspiration, and original innocence, which the shadow had hidden from view. Thus it transforms evil into good without our having to struggle against it.

It does not drive away evil thoughts, but it prevents them

from coming to the surface; not that they never show their faces, but when they do, a better one immediately bars their way.

Nature, said Saint Francis de Sales, produces "leaves and leafy shoots at the same time as she produces grapes; we must constantly cut off the leaves and the unproductive shoots." There are two instruments of purification: suffering, with forces us to detach ourselves from things, and memory, which, once they have abandoned us, forces us to spiritualize them.

8 *The well-spring of life*

Purity penetrates into the innermost recesses of the soul, dissolving the scum of egoism, the accumulations of wrong desires, the mixture of fear, suspicion, and baseness which prejudices had formed in us in spite of ourselves. Purity passes through them, and out beyond. For the pure in heart the world has no murky depths; they penetrate through to the well-spring of life. It may happen that they unblushingly show what others more customarily hide, never dreaming that such things could possibly be revealed to all eyes. But this is because purity adds a sort of radiance to Nature. Purity might be defined both as the absence and the height of reserve.

While most people are amazed to find that purity enables a man to reveal nothing but what might be regarded as his private and personal secret, he himself may well wonder how it could be otherwise, or how anyone could possibly consider his secret anything that he has. Though the pure in heart never indulge in self-display, of them alone it can be said that there is nothing hidden, since for them there is no difference between appearance and reality. What they show us is the perfection of their nature, in all its poise and equilibrium, a perfection which indeed renders it invisible, like God, water, light, and virtue. No thought, action, or particular sentiment of theirs could be different from what it is; they give no impression of incompleteness or inadequacy; it is unimaginable that their past or future could possibly be other than what they were or will be. Or else one forgets these thoughts, actions, and particular sentiments, being conscious of nothing but of the essence to which they bear witness, and from which it is now impossible to distinguish them. The opposite of purity is anxiety, which unfailingly creates a division in the soul; but purity abolishes all strife between the soul and herself. A pure soul is at all times everything that she is. Purity is the quality of the child who freely shows us his inner self, before the process of repression and distortion has set in.

Most men would easily find in their own hearts the purest of impulses if they looked for them, but they will not see or acknowledge them, or act upon them, for they instinctively fear that others will think them naive, and so despise them.

Purity is such a perfect thing, so inherently simple, that it gives no handle to vindictiveness. For the pure in heart, self-knowledge involves no division in the soul. Purity is manifested only in the most commonplace activities, the simplest words, the most natural thoughts. Every situation becomes clear and easy to handle; it would seem that purity has the ability to smooth away all obstacles and all excrescences: the world becomes a limpid mirror in which all the longings of the spirit take shape and are realized.

Purity is easier to maintain in solitude: it is in danger of being soiled by contacts. But the perfection of purity is precisely that instead of seeking to protect itself by keeping apart from the world, it proves its strength and efficacy by passing through all uncleanness in the world without receiving any taint, but rather leaving in its midst its own radiance. Even hostility becomes a new source of strength, a trial which is never long absent.

9 *Watching things come to be*

Purity is a living transparency; it is the property of streams. When we see reality in a pure enough light, we see it coming to be.

Purity is indivisible; any stain on the heart is communicated to the mind and the will. On the other hand, it abolishes the sense of self, and delivers us from every personal preoccupation, laying bare the nature of things, and enabling us to participate in the mysterious act which makes them come to be.

Purity is willing that things should be what they are. Impurity is wishing they are different, and so thinking of them in relation to ourselves, which is to infect them with the worm of falsehood or the worm of covetousness.

The pure in heart do not reject any thing they find in their path; they have no desire to modify it, or to add anything to it. The world opens out before them in all its diversity, arousing their wonder and making reflection unnecessary, but also as a hierarchy within which they feel in tune before ever their will has come into play.

Purity brings us nothing herself, but she enables everything to come to us. She would be loath to cause the slightest ripple on the surface of reality with her breath. She is silent, questioning.

The soul possesses nothing, but can receive all things; to her, everything is an offering and a gift. Blessed are the pure in heart, for they shall see God[4]—but Narcissus had no desire to see anything but himself. He whose heart is pure can receive every gift—but the only gift Narcissus sought was himself.

Impurity is wanting to keep for ourselves goods which are offered to all; by trying to prevent them from slipping through our fingers, we cause them in fact to slip through.

10 *The beauty of pure presence*

Purity is a simple and sublime virtue. It silences the passions, and causes the world suddenly to shine forth with a transparency such as to make us hold our breath for fear of clouding it. Purity is the miracle of naturalness.

The visible appearance of things falls away, like a useless veil. The distinction between reality and knowledge vanishes, as though the most perfect knowledge were still impure: we have the strange impression that we no longer need knowledge, since reality itself is present.

Purity is light. No object is pure in itself, but only by reason of the light that shines upon it. Purity makes everything else visible, whilst remaining invisible itself, for it is but the truth of everything that is. Being so, its presence imparts such transparency to the atmosphere that every object on which our eyes alight seems to emanate from it instead of breaking through it.

In purity, things and their meaning are one. Their faces become familiar, and yet we seem to be discovering them for the first time; and we are surprised to find that in their presence we feel no surprise. All things stand once more in the nakedness of their primeval innocence as if, without showing us his face, God were making himself visible in the gifts he gives us.

The real is always pure. Only self-love, in other words our misuse of things, distorts their natural purpose, and makes the finest impure. Purity reduces every thing to its essence; it lays bare what makes it be; it discloses its point of conformity to the will of God. And so there opens out before our eyes a secret and beautiful world, which till then we scarcely dared to imagine could exist; purity seems able of itself to create it, and to dissipate the disorderly world in which heretofore we thought we lived, like an obscure and insubstantial dream.

The finest art is also the purest. It is that which transcends and abjures all showy cleverness; it renders invisible truth visible. It endows the humblest things with an incomparable spiritual depth, and the deep ones with simplicity and naturalness.

Nothing is beautiful which is not pure, but purity beautifies all things. It is indeed the measure of their value. By stripping off all the coverings that are foreign to their essential nature, and so hide it and distort it, it reveals it in its plenitude, as can be seen in such expressions as "pure understanding," "pure will," "pure love." A pure soul is the only one capable of receiving into itself the beauty of light and of love.

The pure in heart see all things in their essential simplicity. Not that they subtract anything from reality; rather, they grasp it in its unity, adding nothing: since anything else must come from ourselves, it cannot fail to pervert and corrupt it. They do not abstract, eliminate, pick and choose—the unity of all reality dwells in them. This is infinity present to the soul, and not susceptible of analysis.

11 *The pinnacle of the soul*

No one can find a meaning to life, or even be willing to live, unless he has reached, at one time or another, the mountain-peak of consciousness, where we would like forever to hold our thinking and our will, and whence we ought in fact never to let them descend. The memory of that hour returns to the mind, heavy with regret and hope, and gives us courage at those moments when we lack the strength to undertake the ascent. No one can hope to abide there continually unless he has adopted as an inflexible rule of conduct the determination to resist unworthy allurements, futile and idle conversations, and the thoughts infected by *amour-propre*, which inevitably creep in along with some care burdening the mind or some desire distracting the attention. Even so, this rule is insufficient in itself: one could observe it faithfully, and yet remain in a state of languor and spiritual drought. The peak of consciousness is a shining pinnacle which we can attain only through our purest activity. The least speck of dust is sufficient to blunt it and to dull its brilliance. Nor is it an assured and permanent resting-place for the soul, which soon slips back once more; and yet it is here alone that she finds the equilibrium which alone can satisfy her, an equilibrium which is at once the most perfect possible, but also the most unstable.

Again, it is at such moments that, by a sort of paradox, our consciousness is filled to capacity. Each of the faculties of the soul is exercised, and all are harmonized; and the conflicts between them which were formerly an obstacle, now add force and ease to the functioning of each. The supreme tension within is now one with that supreme relaxation which brings us into the very presence of things; the most humble among them stands before us, sharply defined, and bathed in supernatural light. Our intent is now so simple and so straightforward that things soften to our touch, and seem to take on a meaning which is itself the accomplishment of that intent. The world becomes transparent to its depths, while the essence of the self becomes limpid too; and the two brightnesses are one. The soul is now so superior to her states that it seems to her they can trouble her no more.

It follows that it is in the present that the peak of our consciousness is to be found. But we are incapable of remaining there. We make excuses: the present moment, we say, offers insufficient matter for thought and action, and so we are forever running away from it. We try to forget that it demands too much effort and too much courage, and we turn aside as our wills weaken, allowing a less enduring but more accessible object to distract us. This we seek either in the past or in the future, in other words, in memory, or in dreams.

The present moment is a peak whence the world opens out before us like a landless ocean, where there is no haven we will reach one day, nor any path leading to a mysterious, far away, and ever-receding distance. Infinity is the negation of the end, and therefore of the way. It is itself the end, and the way. And the soul finds her equilibrium and her security only when she fixes her eyes on infinity present here and now, and has ceased to relegate it to an eternal beyond.

Notes

1. Lavelle says somewhere: "*philosopher, c'est platoniser.*" For him, as for Plato, ultimate reality is the inwardness of things, not their appearance, which is dependent on the physical senses of the perceiver, and which, like the perceiver's body, will pass away. The knowledge of the inwardness of things, which Plato called "ideas," and Lavelle their "*intimité*" or their "*intériorité*," is, both for Plato and Lavelle, the only true goal of philosophy and, in a sense, of life.

2. Fr. *intimité*.

3. Lavelle's adaptation of Matt. 6:22.

4. Matt. 5:8.

AUTHORS

࿔

GENERAL INDEX

G

Genius 124–5, 127, 165–9

Gentleness 147, 173, 182–6, 211

God 16, 34, 72, 73, 84, 88, 113,
123, 124, 131, 146, 165, 191,
192, 216, 218, 219

Grace 79, 104, 117, 136, 175, 179,
184, 202, 214

Gyges 64

H

Habit 187

Haste 177

Hate, Antipathy, Enmity,
Hostility 139–46, 155, 160,
169–71, 182, 217

Heaven 192

Hell 192

Hermes 36

Heroism 189, 203

Holiness 189, 203

Hope 133, 179, 205, 220

Humiliate, Humiliation 171, 203

Humility 137, 146–9, 164, 179,
182, 194

I

Ideas (Platonic) 207, 222n.

Immortality 179

Indifferent, Indifference 107-15,
145, 163, 179, 185, 186

Individual, Individuality 51, 94,
105, 109, 110, 113, 123, 126–9,
136, 137, 168, 171, 182, 209,
210, 214

Infinite, Infinity 54, 135, 144,
178, 193, 197, 198, 202, 220,
221

Initiative 26, 48, 51, 180, 209

Innocence, Innocent 67, 144, 164,
196, 215, 219

Instinct 192–4, 200

Intelligence 95, 98, 99, 100, 133,
140, 170, 201

Intimité 20–1, 44, 71, 100, 134,
164, 201, 210, 222n.

Introspection 43, 52, 66

J

Joy 16, 94, 104, 124, 135, 150, 151,
164, 180, 182, 212, 213, 214

Justice 79, 114, 171

K

Know 44, 53

Knowledge (*see also*
Self-knowledge) 47, 50, 52,
53, 55, 70, 141, 178, 194, 205–
10, 213, 218–19

L

Liberty 21, 47, 51, 65, 86, 113,
126, 136, 166, 176, 211, 214

Light 134, 161, 168, 172, 175, 178,
181, 185, 187, 194, 199, 202,
207, 208, 212–13, 216-19

Love (*see also* Self-love) 26–7, 31,
34, 35, 36–40, 48, 54, 55, 73,
83, 93, 94, 110, 111, 114, 126,
155, 161, 165, 166, 169–70,
175, 177, 186, 191, 194, 201,
210–13, 219–20

Lucifer 34

M

Matter, Material 79, 81, 83, 134,
137, 151, 152, 153, 171, 172,
177, 203, 205, 210, 211, 213